American Book Company's

MASTERING THE GEORGIA 2ND GRADE CRCT IN READING

ALIGNED TO THE GEORGIA PERFORMANCE STANDARDS (GPS)

Mallory Grantham
Jason Kirk

Project Coordinator: Zuzana Urbanek
Executive Editor: Dr. Frank J. Pintozzi

Reviewer: Dr. Karen H. Michael

AMERICAN BOOK COMPANY
PO BOX 2638
WOODSTOCK, GEORGIA 30188-1383
Toll Free: 1 (888) 264-5877 Phone: 770-928-2834
Toll Free Fax: 1 (866) 827-3240
Web site: www.americanbookcompany.com

ACKNOWLEDGEMENTS

The authors would like to gratefully acknowledge the formatting contributions of Marsha Torrens, as well as the graphics expertise of Mary Stoddard and Charisse Johnson.

Copyright ©2009 by American Book Company
PO Box 2638
Woodstock, GA 30188-1318

ALL RIGHTS RESERVED

The text of this publication, or any part thereof, may not be reproduced or transmitted in any form or by any means, electronic or mechanical, including photocopying, recording, storage in an information retrieval system, or otherwise, without the prior written permission of the publisher.

Printed in the United States of America
05/09

Table of Contents

Preface v

Diagnostic Test 1
Evaluation Chart 16

Chapter 1 Why Authors Write 17
Why Do Authors Write? 17
    To Explain 18
    To Teach 21
    To Describe 23
    To Entertain 26
Chapter 1 Review 29

Chapter 2 Genres 33
Stories 33
Fables 36
Folktales 38
Poems 41
Informational Texts 45
Chapter 2 Review 48

Chapter 3 Parts of a Story 53
Who Is in the Story? 53
Where Does the Story Happen? 57
What Happens in the Story? 60
Chapter 3 Review 65

i

Chapter 4 Fact and Fiction — 69
Inferences 72
Chapter 4 Review 74

Chapter 5 Main Ideas and Details 77
Main Idea 77
    Finding Information Quickly 79
Details 82
Chapter 5 Review 84

Chapter 6 Understand What You Read — 87
Ask Yourself 87
Summarizing 89
Chapter 6 Review 93

Chapter 7 What Will Happen Next? — 97
How to Predict 98
    What the Passage Tells You 98
Chapter 7 Review 103

Chapter 8 Cause and Effect — 107
What Happens and Why? 107
    How to Find Cause and Effect in a Story 109
Chapter 8 Review 112

Chapter 9 Graphics — 115
What Are Graphics? 115
Illustrations 116
Charts 121
    Pie Charts 121
    Line Charts 122
Diagrams 124
Chapter 9 Review 126

Chapter 10 Graphic Organizers — 131
Sorting 131
    Venn Diagram 132
    Baskets 133
Time Order 135

    Timeline 135
    Story Train 136
  Chapter 10 Review 139

Chapter 11 Learning Words   145
Context Clues 145
Same Words, Different Meanings 148
Look It Up! 150
    Dictionary 150
    Glossary 152
    Thesaurus 153
Chapter 11 Review 154

Chapter 12 Word Roots   157
Roots 157
Compound Words 161
Chapter 12 Review 166

Chapter 13 Other Word Parts   169
The s Rule 169
    How Many Are There? 169
    Words That Do Not Use the s Rule 173
Other Word Endings 175
    How Do They Compare? 175
        The er Ending 175
        The est Ending 176
        The ly Ending 176
    When Does It Happen? 178
        The ing Ending 178
        The ed Ending 178
        The s Ending 178
    More Rules about Endings 181
Chapter 13 Review 183

Chapter 14 Word Meaning   187
Synonyms 188
Antonyms 191
Homophones 194

Homographs 195
Chapter 14 Review 198

Practice Test 1   **203**

Practice Test 2   **217**

Index   **229**

Preface

Mastering the Georgia 2nd Grade CRCT in Reading will help students who are learning or reviewing the GPS standards for the **Georgia 2nd Grade CRCT in Reading**. The materials in this book are based on the GPS standards as published by the Georgia Department of Education. This book is written to the grade 2 level, corresponding to approximately 300L to 500L on the Lexile text measure scale.

This book contains several sections:

1) General information about the book itself

2) A diagnostic test

3) An evaluation chart

4) Fourteen chapters that teach the concepts and skills needed for test readiness

5) Two practice tests

Standards are posted at the beginning of each chapter, in the diagnostic and practice tests, and in a chart included in the answer manual.

We welcome your comments and suggestions. Please contact us at

American Book Company
PO Box 2638
Woodstock, GA 30188-1383

Toll Free: 1 (888) 264-5877
Phone: (770) 928-2834
Fax: 1 (866) 827-3240
Web site: www.americanbookcompany.com

Preface

About the Authors:

Mallory Grantham is an ELA writer and copy editor at American Book Company. She completed her Bachelor of Arts in English at Kennesaw State University. As a teaching assistant, she led lectures, created lesson plans, graded and edited papers, and evaluated student progress. In addition, Mallory has taught sign language and tutored students in English and mathematics.

Jason Kirk, copy editor and ELA writer at American Book Company, graduated from Kennesaw State University with a bachelor's degree in English. In addition to writing social studies articles and short fiction, he has tutored college writers and worked in both middle and high school English classes.

About the Coordinator:

Zuzana Urbanek serves as ELA Curriculum Coordinator for American Book Company. She is a professional writer with twenty-five years of experience in education, business, and publishing. She has taught a variety of English courses since 1990 at the college level and also taught English as a foreign language abroad. Her master's degree is from Arizona State University.

About the Reviewer:

Dr. Karen H. Michael has been teaching for seventeen years. Dr. Michael completed her doctorate at Purdue University in 2002 in literacy and language education. Since 2000, she has been an assistant professor in the Tift College of Education at Mercer University. She has four publications and has made over twenty-five presentations at local, regional, and international conferences. Dr. Michael has trained many elementary and middle school language arts/reading teachers in Georgia, South Carolina, and Indiana through professional development courses.

About the Executive Editor:

Dr. Frank J. Pintozzi is a former Professor of Education at Kennesaw State University. For over twenty-eight years, he has taught English and reading at the high school and college levels as well as in teacher preparation courses in language arts and social studies. In addition to writing and editing state standard-specific texts for high school exit and end of course exams, he has edited and written several college textbooks.

Test-Taking Tips

1. Complete the chapters and practice tests in this book.

2. Before the test, get a good night's sleep. Eat a good breakfast the next day. Find your classroom, and get settled.

3. Think success. Keep your thoughts positive. Tell yourself you will do well on the test.

4. Read the directions carefully. If you don't understand them, ask your teacher for help.

5. Some people like to look at questions and answers first. Others prefer to read the passage before looking at the answers. Decide which way works best for you.

6. If you are not sure of an answer, take a guess. Get rid of choices that are definitely wrong. Then, choose from the answers that are left.

7. Use your answer sheet correctly. Make sure the number on your question matches the number on your answer sheet. If you need to change an answer, erase it completely.

8. Check your answers. Look over your exam to make sure you have chosen the best responses. Change answers only if you are sure they are wrong.

Georgia 2nd Grade CRCT in Reading Diagnostic Test

This diagnostic test is based on the Georgia Performance Standards for Reading and adheres to the sample question format provided by the Georgia Department of Education for the Reading Criterion-Referenced Competency Test.

Today, you will be taking a test that is like the CRCT. Your teacher will tell you how to mark the answers.

Here are some things to remember:

1. Read each passage carefully.

2. Read each question or sample. Then, choose the best answer.

3. Choose only one answer for each question. If you change an answer, be sure to erase your old answer completely.

4. Don't spend too much time on one question. If you do not know an answer, come back to it at the end.

5. After taking the test, you or your teacher should score it. There is a chart after the test to help you. It will show you what you know and what you need to study.

Diagnostic Test

First, read each passage on your own. Then, read the questions. You should choose the best answer for each question.

Lisa's Left Foot

Lisa always tripped over things. She fell down a lot. Her parents said she was clumsy. She did not care. She smiled and got back up again.

One day, Lisa and Susan were walking home. Lisa did not see the branch in the way. She tripped and fell. This time she wanted to cry. She hurt her left foot.

It hurt very much. Susan helped her get up. She helped Lisa get home. Lisa's foot was big and puffy. Her mom said it was swollen.

Lisa had to go to the doctor. He took an X-ray to see if anything was broken. She broke her left foot. She had to get a cast on her foot. She can't walk on her foot for eight weeks. Lisa says she will be more careful from now on.

Read this sentence from the story.

> She had to get a cast on her foot.

1. What does the word <u>cast</u> mean in this sentence?

    A a hard bandage

    B people in a play

    C a quick glance

2. What word describes Lisa?

    A clumsy

    B smart

    C strong

3 **What part of her body does Lisa hurt?** ELA2R4 i
   A hand
   B nose
   C foot

4 **How long does Lisa have to wear a cast?** ELA2R4 d
   A six weeks
   B eight weeks
   C twelve weeks

5 **What will Lisa MOST LIKELY do in the future?** ELA2R4 b
   A watch where she is walking
   B run as fast as she can
   C never leave her house

6 **What is the OPPOSITE of the word <u>left</u>?** ELA2R3 c
   A east
   B right
   C down

7 **Why does the doctor need to take an X-ray?** ELA2R4 k
   A to see if why Lisa trips
   B to see if Lisa has grown
   C to see if anything is broken

Diagnostic Test

The Dancing Monkeys

by Aesop

A prince trained some monkeys to dance. The monkeys were the best students. They were able to copy dances very well.

The prince liked to dress them in rich robes and masks. The monkeys could dance well. They were as good as any of the servants. Everyone loved the monkeys. Or did they?

There was a sneaky servant who did not like the monkeys. One day, he took a handful of nuts from his pocket. He threw the nuts on the stage.

The monkeys saw the nuts and wanted to eat them. They forgot to dance. They pulled off their masks and robes. The monkeys fought for the nuts.

The <u>dancing</u> came to an end. The people made fun of the monkeys. The prince learned that some things you see are not what they appear to be. The monkeys looked like servants. But they were still just wild animals.

8 This story is an example of

A a poem.

B a fable.

C nonfiction.

9 How would you sum up what the servant did to the monkeys?

A He tricked them into fighting with each other.

B He was nice to the monkeys and helped them.

C He told the prince to fire the monkeys.

10 What is MOST LIKELY the author's purpose in writing this story?   ELA2R4 o

   A to teach that looks can lie

   B to explain why monkeys like nuts

   C to describe the prince's party

11 How many word parts does the word <u>dancing</u> have?   ELA2R4 p

   A 1

   B 2

   C 3

12 What are monkeys MOST LIKELY to do in real life?   ELA2R4 f

   A wear masks

   B live in a castle

   C fight over food

Diagnostic Test

13 Which illustration fits this story BEST?

A

B

C

The Candy Survey

Jesse wants to do a survey. He likes to ask people questions. He decides to ask his friends. He wants to know what candy they like to eat. He thinks that would be a fun thing to know. So, he asks all of his friends.

Jesse goes to Brad and Amy. "What <u>kind</u> of candy do you like?" he asks.

"I like chocolate bars," Amy says.

"I like gummy bears," Brad says.

Jesse writes down their answers. He asks all the kids in his class.

Then he makes a chart so everyone can see the answers. He will tell his class what he found. The chart will help them see and understand the results.

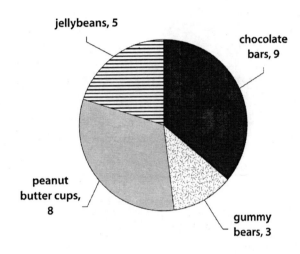

14 In the story, who likes gummy bears?

A Amy

B Brad

C Jesse

15 In this story, what does the word <u>kind</u> mean?

A nice to people

B type of thing

C almost

Diagnostic Test

16 Why does Jesse want to do a survey?   ELA2R4 k

   A He likes to ask questions.

   B He likes to make charts.

   C He likes to eat candy.

17 How many MORE people like peanut butter cups than jellybeans?   ELA2R4 g

   A 2

   B 3

   C 4

18 Which candy do Jesse's friends like the MOST?   ELA2R4 g

   A jellybeans

   B gummy bears

   C chocolate bars

19 Which candy did Amy like?   ELA2R4 i

   A peanut butter cups

   B chocolate bars

   C gummy bears

Georgia 2nd Grade CRCT in Reading

Let's Play a Game!

Sarah was bored. She did not have anything to do. She decided to ask Reese and Adam to play. They brought along some more friends. Soon, they had a big group of kids!

They decided to play hide-and-seek. Since it was Sarah's idea, she got to be "it." She stood by the tree and closed her eyes. She began to count to fifty. "Ready or not, here I come!" she yelled.

She searched all around the yard. She found Adam in a tree. She found Reese and her sister in the doghouse. She found Jerry behind the gate.

Where was James? Sarah looked all over. Then, she heard a laugh. It was coming from the side of the house. She ran over there. "I got you!" she said. James laughed some more.

"Okay, let's play again!" he said.

20 Where do the kids play hide-and-seek?   ELA2R4 l

A the park

B the yard

C the barn

21 Which word sounds the same as the word there?   ELA2R3 c

A their

B were

C here

22 What will MOST LIKELY happen next?   ELA2R4 b

A James will quit playing.

B James will help Sarah.

C James will be "it" next.

Diagnostic Test

23 Where does Sarah find Jerry? ELA2R4 d

A in the doghouse

B behind the gate

C by the house

24 Why does Sarah get to be "it"? ELA2R4 k

A It is her idea to play.

B She asks to be "it."

C No one else wants to be "it."

25 What is the BEST way to sum up this story? ELA2R4 e

A Sarah and her friends play a game.

B Sarah and her friends do arts and crafts.

C Sarah and her friends go to school.

Paper

People write on paper. This book is made of paper.

Most paper comes from trees. People who make paper take the wood from the trees and grind it up. Then, they mix it with water. Next, they add in chemicals. The mix is called "paper pulp."

Sometimes, they add dyes to the pulp. This makes colored paper. They press the pulp down hard to make thin sheets. The paper sheets <u>dry</u>. Then, they are cut.

Paper does not always come from trees. Some paper is made from fibers pressed together. They can be cotton or linen. These are also used to make clothes.

Other times, new paper is made from used paper. This is called recycling.

26 **Why did this author MOST LIKELY write this passage?**   ELA2R4 o

A to explain how to write on paper

B to explain how paper is made

C to explain why paper is important

27 **Which sentence is true about this passage?**   ELA2R4 f

A Paper is not always made from trees.

B People never recycle paper.

C Paper can be cut before it is dry.

28 **How can you tell this passage is nonfiction?**   ELA2R4 m

A It teaches you about paper.

B It has a funny plot about paper.

C It has made-up people who make paper.

Read this sentence from the passage.

| The paper sheets dry. |

29 **Which sentence uses the word dry the same way?**   ELA2R3 b

A Billy is known for his dry humor.

B This song is so dry and boring.

C The ship docked on dry land.

30 In this story, what is one fiber that is NOT used to make paper?

A cotton

B silk

C linen

The Cold

The wind blows;

The doors close.

The cold stays out.

The fire burns;

The log turns.

But, the cold stays out.

The heat stays on,

The chill is gone.

And, the cold stays out.

We do our best

To get some rest,

While the cold stays out.

Georgia 2nd Grade CRCT in Reading

31 What is the MOST LIKELY cause of the cold?   ELA2R4 k

A People are outside.

B There is no fire.

C It is winter.

32 What will MOST LIKELY happen next?   ELA2R4 b

A They will go swimming.

B They will go to sleep.

C They will bake a cake.

33 What is one clue that this passage is a poem?   ELA2R4 m

A It gives facts about heat.

B Some words rhyme.

C It is long.

34 Which word has an ending to make it mean "more than one"?   ELA2R4 p

A coats

B close

C stays

35 How would this poem BEST be summed up?   ELA2R4 e

A Someone is trying to stay happy.

B Someone is trying to stay dry.

C Someone is trying to stay warm.

Diagnostic Test

The New Girl

Madison and Ashlee were very <u>nervous</u>. They could not sit still. They looked at the door. Their teacher said they were getting a new student.

The new boy or girl would be there soon. Madison hoped it was a girl. She wanted a new friend. Ashlee hoped the new person would like her. That is why they were nervous.

Finally, the door opened. The new student came in. It was a girl. She had short hair and glasses. She seemed nice.

Madison and Ashlee smiled at her. She smiled back. The teacher let the class have a snack break.

"What is your name?" Ashlee asked.

"Irene," the girl said.

"I have never heard that name before," Madison said.

"I was named after my grandma," Irene said. The girls talked about names and other things. They were soon good friends.

36 In this story, what does the word <u>nervous</u> mean?

A not angry

B not calm

C not happy

37 Where is this story set?

A bedroom

B lunchroom

C classroom

38 Why did the author MOST LIKELY write this story? ELA2R4 o

   A to describe the day a new student shows up

   B to explain how to be nice to strangers

   C to teach parents how to give names to their kids

39 What does the new girl look like? ELA2R4 l

   A short hair and glasses

   B glasses and long hair

   C tall with long hair

40 Who was Irene named after? ELA2R4 d

   A her mom

   B her grandma

   C her aunt

Diagnostic Test

EVALUATION CHART FOR GEORGIA 2ND GRADE CRCT IN READING DIAGNOSTIC TEST

Directions: On the following chart, circle the question numbers that you did not get right. Then, turn to the chapters, read them, and do the exercises. Review other chapters as needed. Finally, complete the practice tests. They will give you more practice to prepare you for the Georgia 2nd Grade Reading CRCT.

Note: Some question numbers will appear under more than one chapter because those questions require several skills.

Chapter	Diagnostic Test Question(s)
Chapter 1: Author's Purpose	10, 26, 38
Chapter 2: Genres	8, 28, 33
Chapter 3: Parts of a Story	2, 20, 37, 39
Chapter 4: Fact and Fiction	4, 12, 14, 23, 27, 40
Chapter 5: Main Ideas	3, 19, 30
Chapter 6: Understand What You Read	9, 25, 35
Chapter 7: What Will Happen Next?	5, 22, 32
Chapter 8: Cause and Effect	7, 16, 24, 31
Chapter 9: Graphics	13, 17, 18
Chapter 10: Graphic Organizers	13, 17, 18
Chapter 11: Learning Words	1, 15, 29, 36
Chapter 12: Word Roots	11, 34
Chapter 13: Other Word Parts	11, 34
Chapter 14: Word Meaning	6, 21

Chapter 1
Why Authors Write

This chapter addresses the following Georgia grade 2 reading standard:

ELA2R4	a. Reads a variety of texts for information and pleasure. (NOT TESTED)
	o. Recognizes the author's purpose.

WHY DO AUTHORS WRITE?

How do you choose what to read? Some of what you read is nonfiction. That means it is true and tells you facts. You might have to read for school. In science, you may read about what a shark eats.

At times, you read stories. They can be made-up stories. They can be funny too. In English, you may read a story about magic beans. Even when you read for fun, you have a reason to read.

Authors have reasons too. Their **purpose** is their reason for writing. Authors are people who write stories, articles, and so on. You read what they write.

Authors may write to give you ideas or facts. At other times, they may write to make you laugh. When you read, think about it. Why did the author write that passage?

Why Authors Write

Here are some reasons why authors write.

TO EXPLAIN

> Authors write to give you facts.

Authors may write to **explain**. They may tell you how a thing works. You might learn why an event happens. This kind of passage can tell you many facts.

Read this passage.

Turkey Sandwich

Are you hungry for a snack? Let's make a turkey sandwich! You will need two slices of bread. You will also need turkey.

Get the turkey out of the fridge. Put some turkey on the bread. Put the pieces of bread together so that the turkey is on the inside. Then, you can eat and enjoy!

Why did the author write this story?

A to explain how to get a parent's help

B to explain how to make a sandwich

C to explain how to have a good snack

If you picked **B**, then you're right! The author wanted to explain how to make a turkey sandwich.

Chapter 1

Activity: Explain It!

Look at the list below. Choose one thing from this list. Explain it to a friend. You can even draw pictures to help you! Look at the first one, "How to make cereal," as an example.

How to make a bowl of cereal:

First, take a box of your favorite cereal. Open the top.

Pour the cereal into a bowl. Don't spill! Then, get some milk. Pour milk over the cereal.

Then you can get a spoon and eat your cereal!

- How to draw a house
- How to write your ABCs
- How to fly an airplane
- How to color in the lines
- How to be a gymnast
- How to play freeze tag
- How to make a movie
- How to build a fort with blankets
- How to design a dress

Why Authors Write

....

Practice 1: To Explain

ELA2R4 o

Read the story. Then, answer the questions.

Ice Cream Sundaes

Do you like to eat sweets? An ice cream sundae is easy to make. It's also delicious!

Most people like to use vanilla ice cream to start. But you can use whatever flavor you like best. To start, put a scoop of ice cream in a bowl.

Next, you can add toppings. You can choose anything to put on your ice cream. You can put chocolate sauce on the ice cream.

Then you can put sprinkles or nuts on it. Top it off with whipped cream and a cherry. Now that's a perfect sundae!

1 What is the purpose of this story?

   A to explain how to make homemade ice cream

   B to explain how to make an ice cream sundae

   C to explain how to make whipped cream

2 What kind of ice cream does the passage talk about?

   A vanilla

   B chocolate

   C strawberry

3 What topping is NOT talked about in this passage?

   A nuts

   B sprinkles

   C gummy bears

4 In the passage, what can be used to top an ice cream sundae?

   A cherry

   B strawberry

   C apple

TO TEACH

> Authors can write to give a lesson.

Authors can write to **teach** you many things. They may tell you the right things to do. You might read about how a boy helps his friend study. He might do this even if he wants to play instead. He helps his friend because it is the right thing to do.

One writer, Aesop, wrote fables to teach lessons to his readers. You will learn more about fables in chapter 2.

Read this passage.

Look Both Ways

Say you want to play with your friend across the street. You have to cross the road to get there. You should always be careful when you cross the road.

Look to your left. Look to your right. Look to your left one more time. When you are sure there are no cars, you can cross the road. If you follow this advice, you can stay safe!

Why Authors Write

What does this passage teach?

A how to be safe at school

B how to be safe walking home

C how to be safe crossing the road

If you said **C**, then you are correct. This passage teaches us to look both ways before crossing the road.

Practice 2: To Teach
ELA2R4 o

Read the passage. Then, answer the questions.

Listen Up!

Slade was playing a video game in his room. "Slade!" his mom called. "Time for dinner!" Slade was not listening. He was too busy playing. His mom called him again and again.

Finally, Slade's dad came up the stairs. Slade looked up from his game. His dad did not look happy. "Did you hear your mother?" he asked. Slade looked down and frowned.

"No, sir," Slade said. He knew his dad and mom were upset with him. "I will come right now," he said.

"I want you to apologize to your mom for not listening. You also will not play video games for the rest of this week. You need to learn to listen," his dad said.

"Yes, sir," Slade said. Slade looked at his dad. He was smiling. Slade and his dad went downstairs for dinner. Slade apologized to his mom. He promised to listen better.

Chapter 1

1. **What does this story teach?**

   A to listen to music

   B to listen to your parents

   C to listen to your teacher

2. **Why did Slade NOT listen to his mom?**

   A He was playing a board game.

   B He was playing a card game.

   C He was playing a video game.

3. **What was NOT part of Slade's punishment?**

   A He needed to apologize.

   B He had to do the dishes.

   C He could not play games.

4. **What can you learn from this story?**

   A what happens when you do not obey your parents

   B what happens when you do not eat your vegetables

   C what happens when you do not take out the trash

TO DESCRIBE

> Authors describe things so you can picture them.

Some writing can **describe** a person, place, or thing. When you read about it, you can see it in your mind. It may show you how a person looks. It can tell you what a place is like. It may tell you how something feels, tastes, or sounds.

Why Authors Write

Read this passage.

Tigers

A tiger is a big, wild cat. A grown tiger can get very big. It can weigh as much as four adults. That is about as much as eight kids!

You can find tigers in India and China. Most eat meat. This means they are called carnivores.

What does this passage describe?

A tigers

B China

C lions

It looks like it is describing tigers, doesn't it? That's right! Answer **A** is the correct answer.

Activity: Describe It!

Pick a person in your class. Write down things that describe this person. You can talk about hair color. Or you might want to talk about eye color. Say anything you think about what the person looks like.

Read your list to your classmates. See if they can guess who it is! Go around the classroom so everyone gets a turn.

Chapter 1

Practice 3: To Describe
ELA2R4 o

Read the passage. Then, answer the questions.

Brown Thrashers

The brown thrasher is Georgia's state bird. Their bodies are brown and reddish. They have yellow eyes. They have a very long tail. They have curved beaks to help them get food. Thrashers like to eat small insects, nuts, and berries.

Brown thrashers are known for singing beautifully. Some thrashers can mimic other birds.

The brown thrasher builds its nest on or near the ground. Both males and females help to make the nest. Their nests are made out of dried leaves, twigs, and grass.

1 **What is the author's main purpose?**

   A to describe the brown thrasher

   B to describe how birds make nests

   C to describe the mockingbird

2 **What color are a brown thrasher's eyes?**

   A brown

   B red

   C yellow

3 Who puts together the nest?

A males

B females

C both males and females

4 What is one thing that brown thrashers are known for?

A their eating

B their singing

C their flying

TO ENTERTAIN

> Authors write to tell a good story you will enjoy.

What you read can **entertain** you. That means it is fun in some way. It might make you laugh. It could be exciting. It may even be scary.

Some stories are made up. Even real stories can entertain you. You will learn more about kinds of stories in chapter 2.

Read this story.

The Missing Comic Book

Riley was sitting at the lunch table. He had finished eating. He was reading a comic book.

Just then, a loud crash came from the other side of the room. Riley turned around to look. His friend had dropped his lunch tray. He put his comic book down to help.

When he came back, his comic book was gone. Where could it be?

Chapter 1

What purpose did the author have to write this?

A to make readers wonder who took the comic book

B to show how people make loud crashes at lunch

C to give a reason to read a comic book at lunch

The right answer is **A**. Is that what you chose?

Practice 4:   To Entertain
ELA2R4 o

Read the passage. Then, answer the questions.

Nick and Miles

Nick and Miles are puppies. They love to play together. Miles is the leader. Nick follows Miles. They run around the house. They enjoy running up and down the stairs. That is their favorite game.

They also like to bury their bones in the backyard. They take turns hiding the bones. One hides a bone, and the other one has to find it. When they find the bones, they chew them up.

Miles can do lots of tricks. He can sit and stay and roll over. Nick can sit and shake. They like doing tricks. They think it is fun. They get treats when they do a trick.

1 **Why did the author MOST LIKELY write this story?**

A to entertain readers

B to trick readers

C to confuse readers

Why Authors Write

2 Who is the leader?

A Nick

B Miles

C Sam

3 Why do they hide the bones?

A to look for them

B to keep them safe

C to give them away

4 When do they get treats?

A when they bark

B when they bury a bone

C when they do a trick

CHAPTER 1 SUMMARY

Authors have reasons for writing. Those reasons are called their **purpose**.

- Authors write to **explain**. They write to give you facts.
- Authors write to **describe**. They write about things so you can picture them.
- Authors write to **teach**. They can write to give a lesson.
- Authors write to **entertain**. They write to tell a good story you will enjoy.

Chapter 1

CHAPTER 1 REVIEW

ELA2R4 o

Read each passage. Then, answer the questions.

Rachel

Rachel is my best friend. She is short like me. She has red hair that is really curly. Her green eyes are really bright. I really like the color.

She has lots of freckles on her face. She does not like them, but I do. I wish I had freckles.

Rachel is in my class at school. She is very smart. She always knows the right answer. She also sits beside me at lunch.

We play together at recess. Our favorite thing to do is play on the swings. We take turns pushing each other very high.

1 Why did the author MOST LIKELY write this story?

   A to explain how to swing

   B to describe her friend

   C to teach about freckles

2 What color hair does Rachel have?

   A blond

   B brown

   C red

3 What word describes Rachel's eyes?

   A bright

   B dull

   C blue

Go Fish!

Brent and Shelbie were playing Go Fish. Shelbie was winning. She had six pairs. Brent only had four pairs. It was Shelbie's turn.

"Do you have any queens?" she asked.

"Oh man," he said. "This is no fair! You always win!" Brent threw down his cards and ran away. Shelbie ran after him. She sat beside him.

"Please don't be mad at me, Brent. I like playing with you. I do not care if I win or lose," she said. Brent looked at her and gave a little smile.

"I am sorry I got mad at you, Shelbie. Can we play some more?" Brent asked. Shelbie got up and pulled Brent back to the cards. They had a lot of fun.

4 What does this passage teach?

A not to play Go Fish

B not to be a bad loser

C not to give away cards

5 What did Shelbie teach Brent?

A that it did not matter if she won

B that she wanted to win the game

C that he was being a mean friend

Chapter 1

Slumber Party!

Lila was so happy. It was her birthday! She was having a party. She invited her four best friends. They were going to sleep over at her house.

Her dad ordered cheese pizza to eat. Her mom rented *Enchanted*. The girls were going to eat pizza and popcorn and watch movies all night.

They played games and told jokes until it was very late. Then, Macy got sleepy. She curled up in her sleeping bag. Paula yawned and cuddled with her teddy bear. Lila and Diana were tired too.

They had a lot of fun, but now it was time to go to bed. They all agreed they would stay up all night the next time.

6 In this story, the author wants to entertain by writing about

A a movie.

B pizza and popcorn.

C a birthday party.

7 What kind of pizza did the girls eat?

A cheese

B pepperoni

C veggie

8 Which girl had a teddy bear?

A Macy

B Paula

C Diana

Take a Swing

Anthony wanted to play baseball. The only problem was he could not hit the ball. He missed every time! He was very sad that he did not know how to play. So, he asked his older brother to help. Jason said he would help.

He took Anthony outside in the yard. He explained how to hold the bat the right way. He showed Anthony a batter's stance. Finally, Jason said it was time to try to hit the ball. He pitched the ball. WHOOSH! Anthony missed. "It's okay," Jason said. "Try one more time."

Anthony got in his best batter's stance. He held the bat tight. Jason threw the ball. CRACK! Anthony hit the ball! He was so excited.

9 Why does Anthony need Jason's help?

A Anthony cannot hit a ball.

B Anthony cannot throw a ball.

C Anthony cannot catch a ball.

10 What is one thing Jason explains to Anthony?

A how to pitch a curveball

B how to hold the bat right

C how to swing harder

Chapter 2
Genres

This chapter addresses the following Georgia grade 2 reading standard:

ELA2R4	a. Reads a variety of texts for information and pleasure. (NOT TESTED)
	m. Recognizes the basic elements of a variety of genres (e.g., poetry, fables, folktales).

Do you like to read? Maybe you read with your mom or dad. What kinds of stories do you like?

Some stories are real. Some are made up. In this chapter, we will talk about all kinds of stories.

STORIES

You can read many **stories** in books. A story can be made up.

Have you ever read *Charlotte's Web*? In this story, pigs and spiders can talk. A spider writes words. The spider tries to help the pig. In real life, pigs and spiders cannot do these things. This story is made up.

Can you think of any more made-up stories?

Genres

Activity: Make Your Own Story!

Now you can write your own story! Each column has choices. Choose one word from each column. Then, fill in the blanks with your word choices.

Column 1	Column 2	Column 3
How do you feel now?	What do you want to be when you grow up?	What is the best place to visit?
tired	astronaut	the woods
glad	police officer	Florida
gloomy	athlete	the county fair
bored	chef	the movie theater
silly	pilot	Africa
calm	nurse	the game store
lucky	teacher	the ocean

Your Story

Last night, I felt very _____. Then, I had such a fun dream.
          (column 1)

I dreamed that I was a (an) _____. I lived in _____, and all my
                             column 2   column 3

friends lived there too.

I wonder what dream I will have tonight?

You can make as many stories as you want. Pick new words. Then, fill in the blanks again.

Read your stories to a parent or a friend. Or, you can trade with classmates and read what they wrote!

Chapter 2

Practice 1: Stories

ELA2R4 m

Read the story. Then, answer the questions.

Timmy

Timmy magically turned into a bee. He flew to meet his friends Jack and Tina. They were walking to the field. They were going to play baseball.

"Hey, guys. Let's play," said Timmy.

"You're not Timmy. You're a bee," said Tina.

"Bees are bad at baseball," said Jack.

"Turn back into a person, Timmy," said Tina.

Timmy turned into a monkey.

"That is good enough," said Jack.

"I do not think that is good enough," said Tina.

Timmy turned into a person.

"Now can we play?" said Timmy.

1 Is this story about real life or is it made up?

  A real life

  B made up

  C neither

Genres

2 How do you know?

  A Timmy turns into animals.

  B Tina and Jack like baseball.

  C Timmy has two friends.

3 Which part of the story could happen in real life?

  A A monkey could play baseball.

  B Kids could have a friend who is a bee.

  C Girls and boys can play baseball together.

FABLES

A **fable** is a kind of story. A fable is a story that teaches a lesson. Chapter 1 has more about passages that teach lessons.

Aesop is famous for his fables. He wrote many of them. He used animals in his stories. They can talk and think.

Look at this example.

The Turtle and the Rabbit
by Aesop

A rabbit made fun of a slow turtle. The rabbit wanted to race the turtle. The turtle agreed.

They started the race. The rabbit shot ahead. He ran very fast. He saw that he was far ahead of the turtle. He sat under a tree to relax.

The rabbit fell asleep. The turtle walked along. The turtle won the race.

The rabbit woke up. He saw that he had lost.

Chapter 2

What is the lesson in this fable?

A Sleep is for losers. Stay awake.

B Never run fast. You will get nowhere.

C Keep going. You might win.

Think about the story. What does it teach you?

Is it answer **A**? Sleep is not for losers. Sleep is good for you.

Is it answer **B**? In a race, you need to run fast. Running fast can help you win.

If you chose answer **C**, you are right! The turtle is not as fast as the rabbit. But he wins. He wins because he does not give up.

Practice 2:   Fables
ELA2R4 m

Read the story. Then, answer the questions.

The Dog in the Water

by Aesop

A dog walks across a bridge. She carries a bone in her mouth.

She looks down at the water. She sees a dog in the water. It has a bone in its mouth too!

She wants to take the other dog's bone. She growls at it. It growls back.

She makes a mean face at it. It makes a mean face back.

She lets go of her bone. She dives in the water.

She looks around. She does not see the other dog. Her bone has floated away.

Genres

She realizes there was no other dog. It was just her reflection in the water. She was seeing herself when she looked in the water.

1 **Why did the dog jump in the water?**

   A She could swim home faster than she could walk.

   B She thought another dog had a bone.

   C She was hot in the sun.

2 **What lesson should the dog learn?**

   A Do not wait too long.

   B Do not walk on bridges.

   C Do not be greedy.

3 **How can you tell this story is made up?**

   A A dog can't see its own reflection.

   B We can't tell what a dog is thinking.

   C Dogs do not jump into the water.

FOLKTALES

A **folktale** is another kind of story. It tells the story of a group of people. Folktales can be very old.

Some folktales try to explain things that happen. They are made-up stories that tell what MIGHT have happened. They explain things when people don't know what really went on. Here is an example.

Chapter 2

Bumba
A Congolese Folktale

Bumba was lonely. He had a world. But nobody lived on it! The world was full of water. It was all dark. He was sad.

One day, he felt a pain in his belly. He spat up the sun, moon, and stars. They flew into the sky. He spat up again. Trees came out. They landed on the ground. Next came animals. They landed near the trees.

Bumba made the first woman. She gave birth to Woto. He was the first king. Woto soon had many people to watch over. Bumba was not lonely any more. Bumba went to watch from heaven.

This is a very old story. People came up with it to explain how the world began. They made this story up because they did not know. The story is not true, but it was a good guess!

Some folktales are based on real things. Johnny Appleseed is an American folktale hero. He was a real person. He really did travel the country. He really did plant trees all over the place. But some of the stories about him are not true. Not all animals loved him. He did not really plant trees in the sky.

Johnny Appleseed

Genres

Practice 3: Folktales

ELA2R4 m

Read the story. Then, answer the questions.

Con Tiqui
An Incan Folktale

There was no light in the world. All the people were sad. They could not see anything. Con Tiqui popped out of a lake. He wanted to help.

Con Tiqui

He felt bad for the people. He put his crown in the sky. It became the sun. People were happy about being able to see. He told people to explore the world. He showed them how to build things.

Con Tiqui felt better. He went back home to the bottom of the water.

1. How do you know that this is a folktale?

   A The story teaches a lesson.

   B It explains how something happened.

   C It uses talking animals to tell the story.

2. What is true about this story?

   A The ground is next to the water.

   B Someone can live at the bottom of the sea.

   C A shiny crown can become the sun.

3 Why did Con Tiqui feel bad?

A He did not have a crown.

B People could not see.

C People lived under water.

4 Con Tiqui gave the people

A food.

B music.

C light.

POEMS

A **poem** is not the same as a story. A story has sentences, but a poem is written in lines.

A poem can rhyme. Think about the word *long*. Then think about the word *song*. Do they sound the same? This is because they rhyme. They both use the *ong* sound. Some poets like to rhyme words. It makes a poem fun to read.

Read this poem.

Dust of Snow

by Robert Frost

The way a crow

Shook down on me

The dust of snow

From a hemlock tree

Has given my heart

A change of mood

And saved some part

Of a day I had <u>rued</u>[1].

---

[1]To <u>rue</u> means to be sad about something.

Genres

Do you know what this poem is about? It's about nature. It can make people feel good. The speaker in this poem is having a bad day. But he feels happy while watching a bird shake snow from a tree.

This poem also has rhyming words in it.

Which word has the same ending sound as the word <u>tree</u>?
A me
B heart
C crow

If you said <u>me</u>, then you are right. The words <u>tree</u> and <u>me</u> have the same ending sounds. Rhyming words can be fun!

Chapter 2

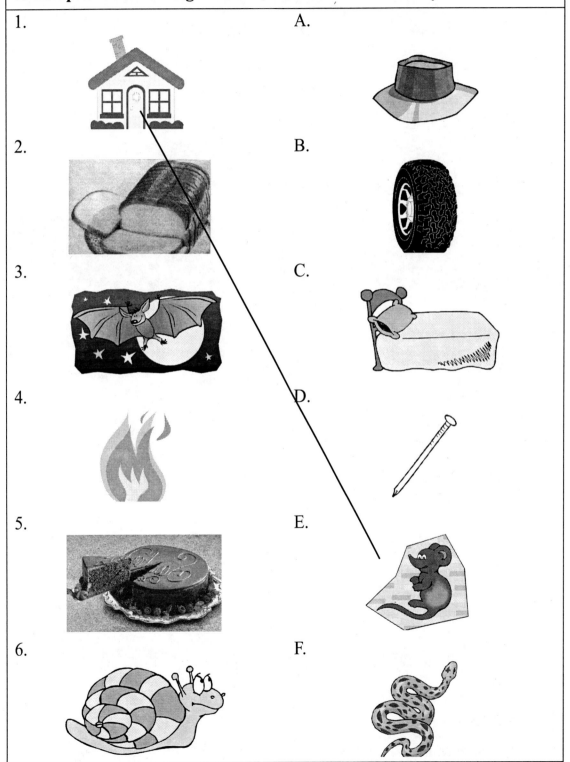

Genres

Practice 4: Poems
ELA2R4 m

Read the poem. Then answer the questions.

The World's Need
by Ella Wilcox

So many gods, so many creeds[1],
So many paths that wind and wind
While just the art[2] of being kind
Is all the sad world needs.

1. The speaker describes the world as being
   A round.
   B sad.
   C warm.

2. Which word would rhyme with <u>needs</u>?
   A near
   B sheds
   C seeds

3. In this poem, the speaker thinks
   A there are not enough roads.
   B people should be nice.
   C the world is too happy.

[1] A creed is a belief.
[2] Art can mean skill.

Chapter 2

INFORMATIONAL TEXTS

A text is what you read. A text that informs is one that tells you facts. So, a passage that informs is called an **informational text**.

Some passages can teach you about a topic. They can help you learn new topics. Think of all the facts you read in your school books. Those are examples of informational texts.

Look at an example.

Worms

Worms live in almost all parts of the world. They even live at the bottom of the ocean. Most live in the dirt.

Worms are good for dirt. They help air go through the dirt. They eat dead plants. This is good for plants. It helps new plants grow.

Worms have been on earth for a long time. They have been around since the dinosaurs. Worms have been good for plants for a long time!

What is this text about? Did you guess worms? You are right! It teaches you about worms. It tells you facts about them. Can you find all the facts about worms?

Genres

Practice 5: Informational Texts
ELA2R4 m

Read the passage. Then, answer the questions.

GPS

Do you know what GPS is?

GPS is a tool that helps people find where to go. Some people have it on their cell phones. It tells them how to get where they are walking. It can find a building anywhere on earth!

Other people put a GPS box in their cars. It tells them which streets to drive on. Even the Army uses it to tell troops where to go. In fact, the Air Force is in charge of GPS.

How does GPS work? Well, you have to be good at math to get it all. But here are the basics:

Your GPS tool sends signals into outer space. These signals reach satellites that are 12 thousand miles away. A satellite is a machine in space that picks up and sends signals. It figures out where you are. It finds where you want to go. It sends signals back. In seconds, your GPS tells you how to get there.

1 Many people have GPS in their

  A cars.

  B hair.

  C shoes.

Chapter 2

2 What is one thing that GPS might NOT be able to find?

A your house

B your neighborhood

C your homework

3 What is this article about?

A facts about the Air Force

B facts about GPS

C facts about outer space

4 How can you tell this is an informational text?

A It teaches you a lesson.

B It tells you facts.

C It rhymes.

CHAPTER 2 SUMMARY

There are many kinds of stories. A **story** can be made up.

- A **fable** is a kind of story. A fable is a story that teaches a lesson.
- A **folktale** is another kind of story. It tells a story written by a group of people.

A **poem** is written in lines. It may rhyme.

An **informational text** gives you facts. It helps you learn new things.

Genres

CHAPTER 2 REVIEW

ELA2R4 m

Read each passage. Then, answer the questions.

The Lion and the Mouse

A mouse was running. She bumped into a sleeping lion and woke him up. The lion was very mad. He put his huge paw on top of the mouse.

"I'm sorry," said the mouse.

"I should hurt you," said the lion.

"No, you should not," said the mouse. "You should let me go. I might be able to help you some day."

The lion laughed out loud. He did not think a tiny mouse could ever help him. He rolled on the ground. He laughed so hard that the mouse walked away.

The next day, a hunter tied the lion with a rope. The lion was stuck! The mouse saw this. She ran to help by chewing through the rope. The lion could move again. The mouse had set the lion free.

"I was right," said the mouse.

"You were right," said the lion.

Chapter 2

1. **Why does the lion get so mad?**

   A The mouse is very small.

   B The mouse wakes him up.

   C The mouse sets him free.

2. **What is the lesson of this story?**

   A Never play with ropes.

   B Walking is always better than running.

   C Everybody needs help sometimes.

3. **Why does the lion laugh?**

   A The mouse is so nice.

   B The mouse is so small.

   C The mouse is so fast.

4. **How can you tell the story is not real?**

   A The lion puts his paw on the mouse.

   B The animals talk to each other.

   C The mouse chews through a rope.

Genres

Fog
by Carl Sandburg

The fog comes

on little cat feet.

It sits looking

over harbor and city

on silent haunches

and then moves on.

5 What about this poem is made-up?

  A Fog does not really look over a harbor.

  B Fog does not really go over cities.

  C Fog does not really have feet.

6 What sits over the harbor?

  A the fog

  B little cat feet

  C the city

7 What is this poem MOSTLY about?

  A the way cats are smart

  B the way the harbor is loud

  C the way fog moves quietly

8 What kind of writing is this?

  A a poem

  B a fable

  C an article

Chapter 2

The Parts of the World

Look at a map of the world. Do you see how some parts look like they could fit together? South America and Africa look like they go together. Do you know why this is?

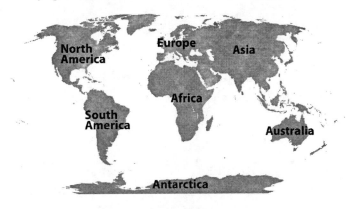

How the Earth Looks Now

It's simple. They used to be a part of the same piece of land. In fact, all the land in the world was one big piece. This was many, many years ago.

How do we know this? Rocks deep in the earth show how it looked. There are also other clues in the ground that prove it. Here is an example:

How the Earth Used to Look

There are some very old bones in the ground in Africa. These bones are from a very old kind of lizard. Bones from the same lizards are also in South America. How are these same bones in two places? Because these two places used to be one place.

Genres

9 The earth used to be one big piece of land. What is one way we know this?

    A Old bones in the ground show it.

    B Somebody saw it happen.

    C It was on the news.

10 A good title for this passage would be

    A "One Big Piece of Land."

    B "Very Old Bones."

    C "Rocks in the Ground."

11 When was all the land in one big piece?

    A a couple years ago

    B yesterday

    C many, many years ago

12 How do you know this passage is an article?

    A It makes up a story about how lizards lived.

    B It gives you facts about the land on the earth.

    C It teaches a lesson about digging up bones.

Chapter 3
Parts of a Story

This chapter addresses the following Georgia grade 2 reading standard:

ELA2R4	a. Reads a variety of texts for information and pleasure. (NOT TESTED)
	l. Recognizes plot, setting, and character within text, and compares and contrasts these elements among texts (NOT TESTED).
	h. Makes connections between texts and/or personal experiences (NOT TESTED).

Think about a clock, a house, or a song. All have many parts. A story has parts too. Each part helps to tell the story. Do you know the parts?

A story has these parts:

- characters
- a setting
- a plot

Read on to learn about each one.

WHO IS IN THE STORY?

A **character** is someone in a story. It can be a person. It can be an animal. It can even be a thing that is not alive in real life.

Characters do things. They make the story happen. They all have traits. Some are tall, and some are short. Some are funny. Some feel sad. Some try to be nice. Some are mean.

Parts of a Story

Some characters do things that cannot happen in real life. Think of the movie *Alvin and the Chipmunks*. They sing and dance. Chipmunks cannot do those things in real life. In a story, they can!

Many characters learn a lesson in the story. They might act one way at the start of a story. Then, they may learn a lesson. At the end of the story, they are different. Most times, it is a good change.

Try to think of characters as people. Think about how they feel. Think about why they act the way they do. They are not all the same. They act and talk in their own ways.

Sometimes, you can compare characters. To **compare** is to see how things are the same. Here is an example:

Pinocchio is a character who lies. He is a wooden puppet. But, he wants to be a real boy. He learns to stop lying. He does become a real boy. His story has a happy ending.

The boy who cried wolf is another character who lies. He is a boy who takes care of sheep. He also learns to stop lying. But, he learns the hard way. He lies so much that no one believes him when he tells the truth. His story does not have a happy ending.

These characters are not from the same places. Their families are not the same. They do not look the same. But, what IS the same about them? They both learn not to lie. That is how we can compare them.

Chapter 3

Activity: Make a Character!

This activity will help you make a character for your own story. Look at the groups of words. Choose which word you want to fit your character. You can also fill in the blanks with your own words.

At the end, you can tell what your character looks like. You also get to pick a name!

Is your character a boy or a girl?	What is your character?	If you picked an animal, what kind is it?
boy	person	anteater
girl	animal	buffalo
neither	thing	chimp
		giraffe
		kangaroo
		tiger
If you picked a thing, what is it?	**How does your character feel?**	**How does your character act?**
bowling ball	excited	helpful
monster	happy	nice
puppet	mad	mean
rock	sad	strong
toast	silly	
toothbrush	sleepy	
Who is your character in the story?	**Describe what your character looks like.**	**What is your character's name?**
good character		
bad character		
funny character		
serious character		
Now, keep this for the next few activities in this chapter. By the end, you will have your own made-up story!		

Parts of a Story

Practice 1: Characters

ELA2R4I

Read the story. Answer the questions after it.

Mrs. Williams

Mrs. Williams is a second grade teacher. She has been teaching for thirty years. That is a long time!

She is a very hard teacher. She is very strict. She has many rules. Some kids think she is mean, but students in her class learn a lot.

One day, her students wanted to do something nice for her. They got some flowers and put them on her desk.

When she came in, she saw them. She started to cry. She was so happy. She did not give the class a quiz that day.

1. What word BEST describes Mrs. Williams?

    A lazy

    B hard

    C boring

2. What sentence is true?

    A Mrs. Williams does not like school.

    B Mrs. Williams likes to play sports.

    C Mrs. Williams loves her students.

Chapter 3

3 What word BEST describes Mrs. Williams' students?

  A kind

  B hungry

  C sleepy

4 Which character changes by the end of the story?

  A Mrs. Williams was mean, but now she is nice.

  B The students were good, but now they are bad.

  C No one changed in this story.

WHERE DOES THE STORY HAPPEN?

The **setting** is a place. It is where a story happens.

A story can be set anywhere. It can be set in a lunchroom. It can be set in another country. It can be set on a spaceship.

As you read a story, think about where it takes place. That is the setting.

Read this passage. Where is this story set?

Kate

Kate is walking outside. There are many food stands with yummy treats.

She can smell hot dogs and popcorn. She sees a roller coaster. She wants to go on all the rides.

Where is Kate in this story?

  A a baseball game

  B the state fair

  C the zoo

Well, this story does not talk about sports. It does not talk about animals either. It talks about rides and food. That sounds a lot like a state fair, right?

Parts of a Story

Some stories are set in the same place. So, you can compare them.

Here is an example:

- The *High School Musical* movies are set in a school. Groups of kids learn to get along with each other. They sing songs and dance.
- The *Harry Potter* stories are also set in a school. Harry Potter learns how to use magic. He trains to fight an evil wizard.

These stories are very different. But they are both set in the same kind of place. This is how we can compare their settings!

Activity: Choose a Place!	
This is the second part to your made-up story. You will now choose a place. Choose which words best fit your setting. Or, pick your own words.	
Where do things happen? inside outside under something on top of something	**If you picked inside, where is it?** a car wash a doctor's office a mall a restaurant
If you picked outside, where is it? a farm a mountain a playground your backyard	**If you did not want any of those, what would you pick?** in another country in another time in outer space under the ocean
Remember to keep this. You will use it for more activities coming up. By the end, you will have a whole story!	

Chapter 3

Practice 2: Setting

ELA2R4 I

Read the story. Answer the questions after it.

A Fun Day

Jill and Dad spend the day together every Saturday. Today, they go to the park. They take their dog, Pinky.

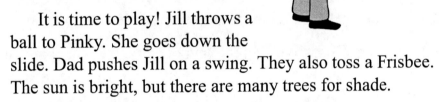

There is green grass all around. There is a playground. There is a fountain in the middle of the park. It shoots water high in the air.

It is time to play! Jill throws a ball to Pinky. She goes down the slide. Dad pushes Jill on a swing. They also toss a Frisbee. The sun is bright, but there are many trees for shade.

Soon, it is time to go home. Jill and Dad stop for ice cream on the way home. Jill cannot wait for next Saturday!

1. **Where are Dad and Jill?**

   A at home

   B at the park

   C at a beach

2. **Pretend Jill and Dad went to the store on the way home. How would this story change?**

   A They could not bring Pinky into the store.

   B They would not have fun.

   C They could not go out next Saturday.

Parts of a Story

3 Can you imagine what this setting looks like? Draw a picture of it. Think about these things as you draw:
- How do Jill and Dad get to the park?
- How many other people are there?
- What does the sky look like?
- What else is on the playground?
- What does the fountain look like?

WHAT HAPPENS IN THE STORY?

A **plot** is what goes on in a story. It is the action.

There are many kinds of stories. But, some stories are about the same things. We can compare them. Take a look at this:

The Lion King is about a son who goes away. He comes back after talking to the ghost of his father. His friends need help. He is able to help them.

Superman Returns is a very different kind of story. It is not about animals. It is about a man who can fly. But, it is also about a son who goes away. He talks to the ghost of his father too. Then, he comes back to help his friends.

As you can see, stories can have plots that are similar.

Plots are not all the same. But, any plot has parts. It has a beginning. Then, it has a middle. Finally, it has an end. Each part has events in it.

This shows the order an event can happen.

Chapter 3

Most stories go like this:

Event	Example
Beginning	
This part shows who the story is about.	Fluffy is a dog. She is sad.
We see the setting.	She wanders around outside.
We see other characters.	Billy the blue jay asks Fluffy why she is sad.
We see the problem of the main character.	Fluffy is lost.

Event	Example
Middle	
The main character tries to solve the problem.	Fluffy tries to find her way home.
Others may help.	Billy flies around, trying to find Fluffy's house.
Some may be no help.	Digger the squirrel does not care that Fluffy is lost. He just wants to play.

Parts of a Story

Event	Example
End	
The problem may be solved.	Billy finds Fluffy's house! It is across the street.
A character may be changed.	Digger feels badly. He says he is sorry he did not help.
We see how the story ends.	Fluffy goes home and gets a puppy treat.

Practice 3: Plot

ELA2R4 I

Read the story. Answer the questions after it.

Math Class

Lucy loves math class. She likes to add numbers. She is good at it.

Joey does not like math class. He thinks math is dumb.

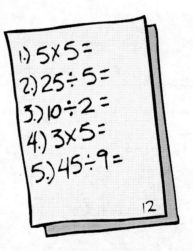

They have to take a math test. Joey did not study for it. He tries to look on Lucy's paper. She gets mad at Joey. She does not want him to cheat. She hides her paper.

The teacher sees Joey looking at Lucy's paper. She calls him to her desk. She gives him a zero on his test. Joey is sad. He knows he should not cheat.

1 Where are Lucy and Joey?

A at Lucy's house

B at school

C at the doctor

Chapter 3

2   What is Lucy's problem?

   A   Joey is trying to cheat off her paper.

   B   She does not know the answers to the test.

   C   She keeps falling asleep in class.

3   How does she solve her problem?

   A   She goes to sleep.

   B   She hides her paper.

   C   She tells on Joey.

4   What word describes the teacher?

   A   boring

   B   sleepy

   C   fair

5   How does the story end?

   A   Joey gets a good grade.

   B   Lucy fails her test.

   C   Joey gets in trouble.

Activity: Make It Up!

Look back at the character you made up. Also look at the setting you picked. Now, write a story about them. It can be very short. It can be funny or sad. Make sure you write about your character. You can add more characters too.

You could even draw a picture to go with your story. Just use your imagination!

Chapter 3 Summary

A **character** is someone in a story.

A **setting** is where the story takes place.

A **plot** is what goes on in a story. The plot goes like this:

- The **beginning** is how the story starts. It tells who is in the story and where it is set.
- The **middle** has many events. It also has a problem.
- The **end** shows how the story ends.

To **compare** is to find things that are alike.

Chapter 3

CHAPTER 3 REVIEW

ELA2R4 I

Read the passages. Choose the best answer for each question. Circle the letter next to the answer you pick.

Robbie and Mark

Robbie and Mark want to practice basketball. They always play at school. But, they do not have a goal at home. So, they decide to make one.

Dad helps them make the goal. He finds a metal rod. He shapes it into a circle. Now, they need a board.

Dad drills holes in a big piece of wood. He shows the boys how to use nuts and bolts. The boys attach the hoop to the board. Now, it is time to paint it.

Robbie wants to paint it red. Mark wants it to be blue. They cannot agree. They fight about the color.

Dad comes up with an answer. They can paint it both colors. Robbie and Mark like this idea.

1. What happens right after Dad shapes the hoop?

   A Dad drills holes in the wood.

   B The boys paint the backboard.

   C Mom calls them in for lunch.

Parts of a Story

2 Who wants to paint the backboard blue?

A Robbie

B Mark

C Dad

3 What is the boys' problem?

A They cannot decide who should make a basket first.

B They cannot decide where to put the basketball hoop.

C They cannot decide what color to paint the backboard.

4 Who fixes the problem?

A Dad

B Robbie

C Mark

5 Where is this story set?

A in outer space

B at the circus

C at their house

Chapter 3

Jimmy Carter

Jimmy Carter is from Georgia. He was born in a city called Plains. He grew up on a peanut farm. He helped make it a good business.

He was the governor of Georgia. Then, he became president of the United States. He is the only president from Georgia.

President Jimmy Carter

He has helped many people since then. He helps people around the world keep peace. He even won an award. It is called the Nobel Peace Prize. He also helps build houses for people who do not have one.

6 What word describes Jimmy Carter?

A unkind

B helpful

C gloomy

7 Say you write a story about Jimmy Carter when he was a boy. Where would it be set?

A Washington

B England

C Georgia

8 What town is Carter from?

A Plains

B Macon

C Jackson

Parts of a Story

9 Which office did Carter hold FIRST?

A governor

B president

C mayor

10 What does Carter do to help people?

A builds boats

B builds houses

C builds schools

Jimmy Carter as a Young Boy in Plains

President Carter in 2009

Chapter 4
Fact and Fiction

This chapter addresses the following Georgia grade 2 reading standard:

ELA2R4	a. Reads a variety of texts for information and pleasure. (NOT TESTED)
	d. Recalls explicit facts and infers implicit facts.
	f. Distinguishes fact from fiction in a text.

Some stories are made up. In chapter 3, you saw some made-up stories. They are called **fiction**. Fiction means "made up."

Others are real. Some real stories are called articles. They have real facts in them.

A **fact** is something that can be proved. You can know facts are true. For example, water turns to ice when it gets very cold. We know this is a fact. How do we know this? Science has showed us this is true.

You have to tell facts (real things) apart from fiction (made-up things). For example, pretend you heard that a day is two hours long. You would know this is not true. How would you know this? You know a day has twenty-four hours!

Take a look at these two statements:

> Sally is a cow.
>
> Sally the cow can talk.

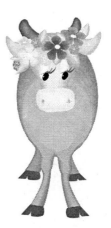

Which is a fact? Which is fiction? From the picture, we can see that Sally is a cow. This is true. This is the fact. Since Sally is a cow, we know she cannot talk. This must be fiction.

In a made-up story, the writer may have Sally the cow talk. But in real life, cows cannot talk. This is how we can tell fact from fiction.

Fact and Fiction

Activity: What Is Real? What Is Not?

Take a look at each picture below. Write one fact about the picture. Also write one made-up sentence (fiction). Use the lines below the pictures. The first one is done for you.

Fact: _Julie is one week old._
Fiction: _Julie is great at math._

Fact: _____
Fiction: _____

Fact: _____
Fiction: _____

Fact: _____
Fiction: _____

Fact: _____
Fiction: _____

Chapter 4

Practice 1: Fact and Fiction
ELA2R4 f

Read the passage. Then, answer the questions.

Carter the Artist

Carter is a mouse. He is a slow mouse. He is not as fast as other mice. He is never in a hurry.

Carter would rather paint. He loves to make art. He paints in his room all day long.

Like all mice, he loves to eat cheese. He also likes to paint pictures of cheese. Other mice like these paintings. They buy them from Carter. He has a pretty good job.

1 Which sentence about Carter is a fact?

   A He is a slow mouse.

   B He loves to make art.

   C He has a pretty good job.

2 Which sentence would MOST LIKELY be made up about a real mouse?

   A He is not as fast as other mice.

   B He loves to eat cheese.

   C He paints in his room all day long.

Fact and Fiction

3 Which sentence could NOT be a fact in real life?

   A Carter sells paintings.

   B Carter is never in a hurry.

   C Carter is a mouse.

INFERENCES

Do you know how you figure out what is a fact? You have this skill already. You just may not know what to call it.

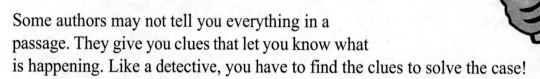

It's called making an inference. When you make an **inference**, you connect what is said and what is not said.

Some authors may not tell you everything in a passage. They give you clues that let you know what is happening. Like a detective, you have to find the clues to solve the case!

But, do not worry. This detective work is easy. Take a look at the next passage.

The Show

   The Ringmaster came out first. He wore a black hat and a bright red jacket. He held a microphone. He said, "Welcome to the Greatest Show on Earth!"

   Then, elephants and monkeys came out and did tricks. They made us laugh. Next, we saw people flying though the air on a trapeze!

Chapter 4

Did you guess this passage is about the circus? You guessed right. The author does not tell us this. So how did you get the answer right?

You looked at the clues to figure out what the passage is about. You looked at the title. You looked at the characters. You looked at the events. You made an inference!

Practice 2: Inferences
ELA2R4 d

Read the passages. Then, answer the questions.

A Great Day

I heard people downstairs. I went downstairs. Mom and Dad were already there. All my friends were there too.

They all said "surprise!" I was so excited. We started playing games and eating cake.

1 What does this passage describe?

A Thanksgiving

B a birthday party

C the first day of school

The Big Yellow Machine

Ann stood on the corner. She waited and waited.

Finally, the big yellow machine stopped in front of her. She got in line. She climbed the steps and found her seat. She was on her way to school.

Fact and Fiction

2 What is Ann waiting for?

   A her school bus

   B her breakfast

   C her dog

CHAPTER 4 SUMMARY

A **fact** is something real.

Fiction is something that is made up.

When you make an **inference**, you connect what is said and what is not said.

CHAPTER 4 REVIEW

ELA2R4 d, f

Read each passage. Then, answer the questions.

Della

Della hurt her foot. She hurt it at the park. It is hard for her to walk.

When she hurt it, she was jumping up and down. She was trying to touch the sun. It took a long time to reach the sun. She tried very hard.

When she touched the sun, it was hot on her finger. She landed wrong. That's how she hurt her foot.

Chapter 4

1 Which sentence is MOST LIKELY made up?

   A She was jumping up and down.

   B She touched the sun.

   C She was trying to touch the sun.

2 Which sentence is a fact?

   A It is hard for her to walk.

   B The sun was hot on her finger.

   C It took a long time to reach the sun.

3 Why does it take Della a long time to reach the sun?

   A Della is not a fast jumper.

   B Della is far from the sun.

   C Della is very short.

Will

Will plays golf. He is not very good at it. But, he cheats a lot.

One day, he plays in a match. The other team's coach watches Will closely. Will cheats the whole time. He pushes his ball closer to the hole. He lies about his score.

"You cheated, Will!" said the other team's coach.

"It's OK. I'm allowed to cheat," said Will.

"Nobody is allowed to cheat. Why would you be allowed to cheat?" asked the coach.

"Because I invented golf in the year 1457," said Will.

Fact and Fiction

4 **What in the story could be real?**

   A Will is not good at golf.

   B Will is allowed to cheat.

   C Will invented golf.

5 **What in the story is made up?**

   A Will cheats a lot.

   B Will wins a match by cheating.

   C Will has been alive since 1457.

6 **Why does the other team's coach watch Will?**

   A He thinks Will is a good golfer.

   B He can tell that Will has practiced.

   C He knows that Will is cheating.

Chapter 5
Main Ideas and Details

This chapter addresses the following Georgia grade 2 reading standard:

ELA2R4	a. Reads a variety of texts for information and pleasure. (NOT TESTED)
	i. Identifies and infers main idea and supporting details.
	n. Uses titles, table of contents, and chapter headings to locate information quickly and accurately and to preview text. (NOT TESTED)

As you can read in chapter 2, there are many types of passages to read.

You can read articles. They have facts. They are meant to inform you. That is why they are called informational texts. You can also read made-up stories. They are not always about real things.

No matter what you read, it has a main idea. It also has details. They tell you more about the subject. Now, we will learn more about main ideas and details.

MAIN IDEA

Everything you read has a **main idea**. This is what the text is about. Articles have main ideas.

Made-up writing has main ideas too. A story has a main idea. A fable has one. Even a poem has one.

In this chapter, we will talk about how to find main ideas.

Sometimes it will be easy to find the main idea. The author may tell you what it is in the story. Here are some tips to help you find the main idea:

77

Main Ideas and Details

- First, read the title of the passage.
- Then, read the entire passage.
- Also, think about what it says.
- Finally, choose what you think it means.

Read this article.

Red

Many objects around us are red. Think of a stop sign. It is red. A red light also tells you to stop.

There are red foods, like tomatoes, strawberries, and some apples.

Some roses are red. Fire trucks are red. When you see a picture of a heart, it is usually red too.

There are plenty of things that are red. Can you think of more?

What do you think is the main idea? This article is about items that are red. Many things are red. That's the main idea!

Chapter 5

FINDING INFORMATION QUICKLY

Sometimes, an author will not tell the main idea. But, you may get hints in the text. In other words, the author will imply the main idea. You have to **infer** what it is about.

We talked about that in chapter 4. Go to that chapter to read more.

Authors help you in many ways to find main ideas. Here are a few ways:

Tool	Example
Titles	**"How to Tie Your Shoes"** – You can be pretty sure that this passage is about tying your shoes.
Table of Contents	Polar Bears . . . . page 2 Grizzly Bears . . . . page 6 Panda Bears . . . . page 10 This table of contents tells you which bear each chapter is about.
Chapter Headings	**Chapter 5** **Main Ideas and Details** This is the chapter heading for the chapter we are working in now. The name of a chapter tells the main idea of that whole chapter.

Main Ideas and Details

It's time for an activity!

> **Activity: What's the Big Idea?**
>
> Write about what you did on your last birthday. Use your own paper. You can draw a picture to go along with what you wrote.
>
> Then, read what you wrote. What is the main idea?
>
> Trade papers with a friend. Try to pick out the main idea in that article. Did your friend find the main idea in yours?

Practice 1: Main Idea
ELA2R4 i

Read the passages. Then, answer the questions.

Ida's School Play

Ida wants to be in the school play. She wants to be Little Red Riding Hood. Tryouts are today. She has practiced her song every day. She is ready.

Ida stands in front of her teacher. She sings "Twinkle, Twinkle, Little Star." Her teacher likes it. She asks Ida about herself. She thanks Ida for coming.

Ida looks at the cast list the next day. She got the part she wanted! Ida is so excited!

1 What is the main idea of this story?

  A Ida likes to sing.

  B Ida's teacher likes her.

  C Ida wants a part in the play.

2 Which sentence about this story is true?

  A School plays are never any fun.

  B Ida practices for the tryouts.

  C Everyone laughs at Ida.

Kyle's Big Mess

Kyle never makes a mess. He keeps his clothes clean. He keeps his room clean. He always knows where his things are.

Today, Kyle tries to make breakfast by himself. He spills the milk. He drops the cereal on the floor. He tries to clean it. But, he gets soap everywhere!

Kyle is afraid his mom will be mad. But, she smiles. "It's all right," she says. "It was an accident."

Kyle's mom knows he is not messy. Every kid can have a bad day! She helps Kyle clean up the kitchen.

3 What is the story MAINLY about?

  A Kyle cannot stay awake in class.

  B Kyle makes a mess one time.

  C Kyle is always busy.

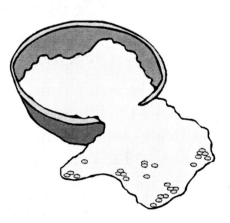

4 What sentence is true about this story?

  A Kyle is a messy person.

  B Kyle is almost never messy.

  C Kyle cannot stay out of trouble.

Main Ideas and Details

DETAILS

Every story has details. **Details** are like pieces of a puzzle. They help make up the whole main idea. They help the main idea make sense.

Details are in a story to make it better. They make the story fun to read. They also give you more to learn.

Here is an example:

> Say a friend asked you about your favorite food. You could just say, "Pizza." Or, you could give more details.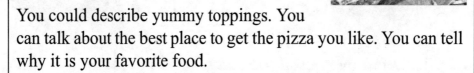
>
> You could describe yummy toppings. You can talk about the best place to get the pizza you like. You can tell why it is your favorite food.

These are all details. The main idea is that pizza is your favorite food. Anything extra you could say is a detail.

Practice 2: Details
ELA2R4 i

Read the article. Then, answer the questions.

Popcorn

Popcorn is a great snack. It is fun to eat when you watch a movie.

Popcorn is not like normal corn. Normal corn on the cob is the kind you have for dinner.

Popcorn is not the same. Each kernel has a small amount of water in it. This makes it explode when it gets very hot. The kernels make a loud "POP!"

Many people like to add butter to their popcorn. Some like salt. There are plenty of flavors to choose. You can even make caramel corn.

There are many cheeses that go on popcorn too. Some people even melt candy and chocolate to mix with their popcorn! Can you think of other toppings to go on popcorn?

Chapter 5

1. **The kernels explode when**
   A they get too soft.
   B they get very hot.
   C they get really cold.

2. **In this article, what do some people like on their popcorn?**
   A salt
   B pepper
   C sugar

3. **What topping is NOT in this passage?**
   A caramel
   B butter
   C hot sauce

4. **Each popcorn kernel has**
   A water inside.
   B caramel inside.
   C chocolate inside.

CHAPTER 5 SUMMARY

The **main idea** is what a story or article is about.

- The author may tell you the main idea. This makes it easy to find.
- If the author does not tell the main idea, you will have to **infer** it.

Details are the smaller parts of a story or article. They help the main idea make sense.

Chapter 5 Review

ELA2R4 i

Read each passage. Then, answer the questions.

Chopsticks

Many people like Asian food. Some eat it with chopsticks. They use chopsticks instead of a knife and fork. Chopsticks are two thin sticks. Some are wooden. Others are plastic.

Using chopsticks may look easy. But, it takes practice. You have to hold them just right.

First, you hold the bottom one like you would hold a pencil. The top stick fits right above it. You only move the top one up and down with your first finger. This looks like you are pinching the air.

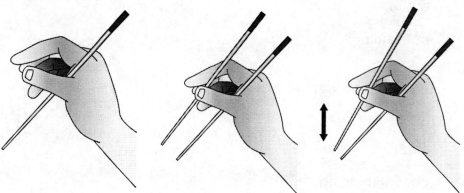

Practice that motion for a while. Then, try to pick up a piece of meat. Be patient. It will take some time. But, don't give up! It's fun to do.

1 What is the main idea of this story?

   A enjoying Chinese food

   B eating with chopsticks

   C holding a pencil

2. In this article, what is one thing chopsticks are NOT made of?

   A metal

   B wood

   C plastic

3. How should you hold the bottom chopstick?

   A like the top stick

   B like a fork

   C like a pencil

4. What are chopsticks used instead of?

   A fork and spoon

   B spoon and knife

   C knife and fork

5. Why is it hard to use chopsticks?

   A They are too long.

   B You have to hold them right.

   C There are many rules for using them.

Mascots

Have you ever been to a sports game? Some teams have a person in a costume. This character walks around during the game. It is called a mascot.

Mascots get the crowds excited. Georgia Tech has a mascot named Buzz. He is a yellow jacket. That is a kind of wasp. He makes the crowd happy. He does pushups after his team scores. The crowd counts along. It is fun to watch!

Mascots are not used only for sports. There are many kinds of mascots. Some companies use mascots to help sell a product. The Trix rabbit is a mascot. You see him on Trix cereal boxes. He is also used on TV.

Some mascots help us learn. Do you know Smokey Bear? He teaches about the woods. He tells how to prevent forest fires. McGruff the Crime Dog teaches about staying safe.

6 What is the main idea of this passage?

A There are many kinds of mascots.

B A rabbit is used for Trix cereal.

C The military uses mascots.

7 Which sentence about this story is true?

A Sports mascots play in the game.

B Sports mascots get the crowd excited.

C Sports mascots never come to the games.

8 What mascot teaches about the forest?

A the Trix rabbit

B Smokey Bear

C McGruff the Crime Dog

9 What kind of animal is Buzz?

A yellow jacket

B rabbit

C bear

Smokey Bear

10 In this story, why do some companies use mascots?

A to bring luck

B to help sell a product

C to show who makes the product

Chapter 6
Understand What You Read

This chapter addresses the following Georgia grade 2 reading standard:

ELA2R4	a. Reads a variety of texts for information and pleasure. (NOT TESTED)
	c. Generates questions before, during and after reading. (NOT TESTED)
	e. Summarizes text content.
	j. Self-monitors comprehension and attempts to clarify meaning (NOT TESTED)

When you read a story or article, you need to know what you are reading. One way you can do this is to ask yourself questions.

You might already do this when you read. This is because you need to know the basics of a story.

- **Who** is in the story?
- **What** happens?
- **Why** do things happen?
- **Where** do they happen?
- **When** do they happen?

On the Grade 2 CRCT Reading test, you will have to answer more questions than just those. There are skills you can learn to help you. This chapter will show you. It will help you learn how to understand what you read.

ASK YOURSELF

You ask questions when you read. **Asking questions** will get your brain thinking about things in the passage. Then, you can answer all the things the test asks you.

Understand What You Read

Look at this example.

James and the Zoo

James likes to go to the zoo. The pandas are his favorite animals. He likes to see the lions and the tigers.

The monkeys are fun to watch. They dance around the trees.

The birds are really cool too. They sing and screech loudly all the time.

James could go to the zoo every day and be happy. There is always something new to see!

Question: Who is this story about?

Answer: James

Question: Where is this story set?

Answer: the zoo

There are many more questions you could ask. Try these:

What animal is James' favorite?

Which animals dance around the trees?

Which animals sing loudly?

Chapter 6

> **Activity: Ask Away!**
>
> **First, look at the story on the page 88. Think about all the questions you can ask. Look at the questions right below the story. On your own paper, list three more questions that you could ask.**
>
> **Now, draw a picture that helps to answer each question.**

SUMMARIZING

One way to understand what you read is to sum up the story. A **summary** tells what you have read in an article or story.

When you sum up a story, you put it in your own words. A summary is usually very short. It gives the main idea. It leaves out the little details.

For example, let's say you have just read "Hansel and Gretel."

A friend asks you what the story is about. Here is a summary you might give of the story:

    Hansel and Gretel get lost in the woods. They find a house in the woods made of candy. They eat food from it and meet the old woman who lives there.

    She is really a witch. Hansel and Gretel are tricked at first.

    But, they find out who she is, so they run away. They find their way home again.

Understand What You Read

> Think about this: Each chapter in this book has a summary at the end. It sums up the things you learned in that chapter.

Read this story. Think about what the BEST summary would be.

Alma

Alma loves to make crafts. She has a special desk in her room to make crafts.

She makes cards and draws pictures. She likes to color. She also puts glitter on everything.

She also makes jewelry with beads. She makes bracelets for all her friends.

What is the BEST way to sum up this story?

A Alma likes drawing pictures.

B Alma likes making bracelets.

C Alma likes making crafts.

The story tells us Alma likes to make crafts. That is the main idea.

Answers **A** and **B** only tell of certain things she makes. Answer **C** is the best. It tells the main idea!

Chapter 6

> **Activity: Sum It Up!**
>
> **A.** Think of the story "Little Red Riding Hood." Try to sum up the story. Remember to put it in your own words.
>
> **B.** Think of your favorite stories. Tell your mom or dad how you would sum it up. Include the main ideas from the story. And try to keep it as short as possible.

Practice 1: Sum It Up
ELA2R4 e

Read the passage. Then, answer the questions.

Troy Goes Fishing

A few times a year, Troy and his dad go fishing. They travel to Lake Allatoona. They spend the whole day together.

Sometimes, they use crickets as bait. Other times, they like to use worms.

Troy enjoys fishing. One day, he caught the biggest fish he had ever seen! Troy's dad was very proud of him.

When they got home, Troy told his mom. She was proud of him too.

1 What is the BEST way to sum up this story?

A Troy goes fishing with his dad.

B Troy likes to use crickets to fish.

C Troy catches bigger fish than his dad does.

Understand What You Read

2 What happened when Troy caught a big fish?

   A His dad was jealous.

   B His dad was proud.

   C His dad was sad.

Flannery O'Connor

Flannery O'Connor was a writer. She was from Georgia.

She wrote many short stories. She wrote about people. Her stories were about how they do the right thing or do the wrong thing. You might read a story by her when you are older.

Peacock

She wrote her stories while she lived on a farm. She had many peacocks. They were her pets. She let them roam around. After she died, the peacocks stayed on the farm.

3 What is the BEST way to sum up this story?

   A Flannery was a writer from Georgia.

   B Flannery was a farmer from Georgia.

   C Flannery had many peacocks on her farm.

4 What did Flannery write stories about?

   A how beautiful peacocks are

   B living on a farm in Georgia

   C people doing right and wrong

Chapter 6

> ## CHAPTER 6 SUMMARY
>
> **Asking questions** can help you understand what you read.
>
> A **summary** is telling a story in your own words.

CHAPTER 6 REVIEW

ELA2R4 e

Read each passage. Then, answer the questions.

Flower Girl

Lena's big sister is getting married. She asks Lena to be her flower girl.

Lena is so excited. She gets to wear a pretty pink dress.

The wedding day comes. Lena wears her dress. She carries a basket of tulip petals. The music starts playing. It's Lena's turn. She has an important job to do.

She walks slowly down the aisle. She tosses the petals to the ground.

Finally, she makes it to the front of the church. She stands in her spot. Lena looks at her sister. They smile at each other.

Understand What You Read

1. What is the BEST way to sum up this story?

    A Lena is a bridesmaid for her sister's wedding.

    B Lena is a flower girl for her sister's wedding.

    C Lena is a guest at her sister's wedding.

2. Which sentence describes Lena's job?

    A She has to walk down the aisle and sing a song.

    B She has to walk down the aisle and gather flowers.

    C She has to walk down the aisle and throw flower petals.

3. What does Lena do when she gets to the front of the church?

    A She drops her basket.

    B She stands in her spot.

    C She runs to her sister.

Football

The kids were crouched down and ready to run.

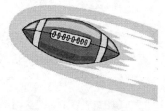

"Hut!" yelled Russell. He caught the football. He looked around for someone to throw it to. He did not want to get tackled. His teammates were trying to get open.

Finally, Russell saw Jacob. He was wide open near the goal line.

Russell was not sure if he could throw the ball that far. He did not think he had ever tried. But, he knew that if he did not throw it, he would get tackled.

Russell took a deep breath. He threw the ball as hard as he could. Jacob reached for the ball. He caught it!

Jacob ran for the goal line. TOUCHDOWN!

Chapter 6

4 How would you sum up the first part of the story?

  A Russell needs to find someone to catch the football.

  B Russell wants to find someone he can tackle.

  C Russell catches the football and makes a touchdown.

5 Which describes what happens when Jacob catches the ball?

  A He gets tackled.

  B He fumbles the ball.

  C He scores a touchdown.

6 Why does Russell think he cannot throw the ball far?

  A He has never tried.

  B He tries and can not.

  C He does not want to try.

The Police Officer

Mrs. Watson is a police officer. She keeps the town safe. She rides around in her police car. She makes sure people stay out of trouble.

When people drive too fast, she has to give them tickets. Then, the people have to pay money.

Officer Watson goes to schools to talk about safety. She teaches kids not to talk to strangers. She also tells them what to do if they get lost.

She asks them questions to see what they learned. At the end of the day, she gives the kids special badges.

Understand What You Read

7 What is the BEST way to sum up this story?

   A Mrs. Watson is a mean person.

   B Mrs. Watson does not like kids.

   C Mrs. Watson keeps people safe.

8 What is one thing that Officer Watson teaches kids?

   A how to talk to strangers

   B stop, drop, and roll

   C what to do if they get lost

9 When Officer Watson teaches, what happens at the end of the day?

   A The kids get badges.

   B The kids get candy.

   C The kids get medals.

10 In the story, what is one part of Mrs. Watson's job?

   A She watches people in jail.

   B She stands in the courtroom.

   C She gives people tickets.

Chapter 7
What Will Happen Next?

This chapter addresses the following Georgia grade 2 reading standard:

| ELA2R4 | b. Makes predictions from text content. |

Think of going to the store with your mom. She picks out noodles and tomato sauce. What do you think you will have for dinner? You might have spaghetti.

Now, imagine you are drawing a picture. You forget to put the top back on the marker. Do you know what will happen? Your marker might dry out. It will probably not color very well.

At times, you do not know what will happen next. You might need to guess. You do this all the time. You might not even realize you do it. Look at these pictures.

What is this man MOST LIKELY building? Pick the best answer.

A a car

B a house

C a tent

97

What Will Happen Next?

Did you pick **B**? That is right! The man is cutting wood. He is also using a hammer and nails. Then, he is laying bricks. A car does not use wood or bricks. A tent is usually made of cloth. They usually don't use wood or bricks either. You can guess the man is building a house.

HOW TO PREDICT

When you looked at the pictures on the page before, you guessed what would happen. This is called **predicting**. You predict all the time.

Do you like to watch cartoons? Did you ever know what was going to happen next? Did you take a guess?

Sometimes you can just know what is going to happen. It might be something in the story. It might be a fact you know.

There are ways to help you predict when you read. This chapter will tell you.

WHAT THE PASSAGE TELLS YOU

You know many people who predict. Have you ever watched people predict the weather?

They predict sunny skies or rain. They use what they know to help them. They also use what they have studied. They have looked at how the weather used to be. This helps them come up with predictions.

When you read a passage, you learn things. You can learn from made-up stories. You can learn facts from articles.

All the things you learn can help you. They can help you predict what happens next. You can use the title and pictures that come with a story or article. These help you understand the story.

Chapter 7

Look at this example.

Family Picture

Amy wants to draw a picture of the people in her house. She has a mom, dad, and two sisters. She starts to draw. She draws her mom and her two sisters.

Who is the next person she will draw?

A her dog

B her dad

C her grandma

Did you guess her dad? That's right! The story is about a picture of all the people in Amy's house. You can use what it says in the text to help you guess the answer.

What Will Happen Next?

Activity: Predict the Weather

Keep track of the weather for a week. Try predicting the weather for the next day. See how well you do!

Here is an example.

Monday

Time: 2:00 p.m. Weather: It is sunny. Some clouds are coming.

Prediction for tomorrow: It might rain.

Tuesday

Time: 10:00 a.m. Weather: It rained this morning. Now it is nice again.

Was your prediction right? Yes, it rained!

Prediction for tomorrow: The day will be sunny.

Wednesday

Time: _____ Weather: _____

Was your prediction right? _____

Prediction for tomorrow:
_____
_____

Now, you try it. Make a page of predictions for the whole week.

Chapter 7

Practice 1: Predicting

ELA2R4 b

Read the passage. Then, answer the questions.

Kevin's Uncle

Every year, Kevin's uncle goes on a trip. His job makes him travel to many places.

He is always gone on Kevin's birthday. Kevin does not mind. His uncle always brings him a gift later.

Today, Kevin's uncle is coming. Kevin is excited to hear about his uncle's trip. He watches his uncle get out of the car. He gets a box out of the back seat. It is wrapped in bright paper. Kevin is excited.

1 Why is Kevin excited?

   A His uncle brought him a gift.

   B His uncle is going on a trip.

   C His uncle did not bring his dog.

2 What is MOST LIKELY in the box?

   A Kevin's homework

   B Kevin's clothes

   C Kevin's present

3 What will MOST LIKELY happen next?

   A Kevin's uncle will go home.

   B Kevin's uncle will give him the box.

   C Kevin's dad will take the box away.

What Will Happen Next?

Julian and His Brother

Julian has a little brother. His name is Toby. He is three years old.

Today, Julian is making a house with his building blocks. Toby wants to help. Julian does not want any help.

Toby gets mad. He kicks the house.

4 What can you predict will happen to the house?

   A It will kick back.

   B It will fall down.

   C It will get bigger.

5 How does Julian MOST LIKELY feel?

   A upset

   B happy

   C tired

CHAPTER 7 SUMMARY

Predicting means guessing what will happen next.

CHAPTER 7 REVIEW

ELA2R4 b

Read each passage. Then, answer the questions.

Halloween Fun

Carly loves Halloween. She enjoys dressing up. One year, she was a princess. Another time, she was a cowgirl. She has worn many fun costumes. But, she cannot decide what she wants to be this year.

She thinks very hard. Her friends try to offer ideas. "Maybe you can be a cat," says Amy. Carly does not like that idea.

"You could be a fairy," Margie says. Carly does not like that idea either. Carly sees a beautiful butterfly. It is pink with black outlines.

Carly smiles. She knows exactly what costume she will wear.

1. What will Carly MOST LIKELY be for Halloween?

    A a fairy

    B a cat

    C a butterfly

2. Which fact helped you make that prediction?

    A She does not like her friends' ideas.

    B She does not have enough money.

    C She smiles when she thinks of a cat.

What Will Happen Next?

3 What will MOST LIKELY happen next?

A She will draw how she wants her costume to look.

B She will not dress up for Halloween this year.

C She will change her mind and be a cat instead.

The Weather

Jon wakes up in the morning and looks outside. It snowed! Jon is very happy. He hopes there is no school.

He goes downstairs. His mom is in the kitchen. She smiles down at him. "I just heard it on the radio," she says. "There is no school today!"

Jon jumps up and down. He gets dressed so he can play outside.

4 What is MOST LIKELY the reason there is no school?

A It is too warm.

B It snowed.

C It is Saturday.

5 What do you predict the weather to be like?

A hot

B cold

C rainy

6 What should Jon put on to go outside?

A a swimsuit

B a suit and tie

C a coat

Chapter 7

Read each passage. Choose the BEST answer for what will happen next.

7 Jimmy held the bat over his shoulder. He made sure he stood over home plate. He looked at the pitcher.

A Jimmy will start singing and dancing.

B Jimmy will swing and hit a ball.

C Jimmy will eat a hot dog.

8 The teacher sat in a chair in front of the class. "All right," she said. "All of you can sit on the floor. Put everything away. Get ready to listen." She opened a book in her lap.

A The teacher will read a story.

B The teacher will give a math test.

C The class will take a nap.

9 Gina took the tray to a table. Her friends were sitting near her. She opened her milk and put a straw in it. She unwrapped her sandwich.

A Gina will do her homework.

B Gina will play outside.

C Gina will eat lunch.

What Will Happen Next?

10 Tyler and Hanna had their new swimsuits on. The sun was warm. They ran toward the beach.

"Bet I'll get there first!" Tyler yelled.

"No, I'll beat you!" Hanna yelled back.

A They will go swimming.

B They will catch the school bus.

C They will play a game of basketball.

Chapter 8
Cause and Effect

This chapter addresses the following Georgia grade 2 reading standard:

| ELA2R4 | k. Identifies and infers cause-and-effect relationships. |

WHAT HAPPENS AND WHY?

Cause and effect is about what happens and why. Have you ever asked "Why?" That is an easy question to ask.

Why do cars have to stop at red lights? Why do dogs chase cats? Why are carrots good for you? There are so many questions to ask.

What you want to know is why things happen. A **cause** is the reason why it happens. This helps you see the effect. An **effect** is result of a cause.

Think about this: Everyone is making gifts for your cousin. You wonder why. You remember that her birthday is next week.

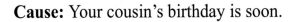

The cause is her birthday. The effect is people making her gifts.

Cause: Your cousin's birthday is soon.

Effect: Her friends and family are making gifts for her.

Now think about this one. What could be the cause?

Cause: _____

Effect: The boat sinks.

    A The boat turns left.

    B The boat has a leak.

    C The boat has a person on it.

Cause and Effect

Did you pick answer **B**? If so, that's right! A leak can make a boat sink. Answers B and C do not work. Boats can turn left and not sink. And boats can carry people and not sink.

Activity: Cause and Effect

Look at the pictures. In each row, the first one is a cause. The other three are possible effects. You pick what will happen. Put a check mark by the one that is the best effect. The first one is done for you.

Cause	A	B Effect	C

Now you know how to spot cause and effect. You can see how they relate to each other.

108

Chapter 8

On the CRCT Reading test, you will find them in a story. We will look at a story now.

How to Find Cause and Effect in a Story

HINT
Think about the order of events.
Read the story.
Think about what event happens first.
Then, think about the result of that event.
Now, you can see which event is the cause.
When you find the cause, you can see the effect.

Here is an example. Look at this part of a story.

Paul

Paul paints a picture. He sells it for twenty dollars. Now, he can buy things because he has money. He buys more paint. As a result, he can paint many pictures.

Do you see the causes and effects? Each event leads to the next event. Here are some questions you may see. Try to answer each one.

- What does Paul do with the first picture he paints?
- How does Paul get money?
- What does Paul do with his money?
- How does Paul get more paint to make more pictures?

Cause and Effect

HINT
Look for key words. There are words that show cause and effect. Look for them in a story. Here are some:
as a result   if … then   so that
because   in order to   this is why
due to   so   this is how

Look at the story about Paul again. Do you see the key words? Here they are. They have lines under them.

> Paul paints a picture. He sells it for twenty dollars. Now, he can buy things <u>because</u> he has money. He buys more paint. <u>As a result</u>, he can paint many pictures.

Practice 1: Cause and Effect
ELA2R4 k

Read the story. Then, answer the questions.

The Pool

It's hot outside today, so we want to go swimming. Mom says she will take us.

First, we find our swimsuits. Next, we get towels. Then, we put on sun block.

We walk to the pool. There are no people at the pool. That means we get to swim more.

There is one problem. There is no water in the pool!

Chapter 8

1. **Why do the kids get their towels?**

    A They are going to sell their towels.

    B They are going to wash and dry a car.

    C They will need to dry off after they swim.

2. **Why are there no people at the pool?**

    A It is not hot outside today.

    B The pool is not open yet.

    C Nobody likes to swim in pools.

3. **Because there is no water in the pool, the kids**

    A cannot swim.

    B swim faster.

    C know how to swim.

4. **What key word in this story shows cause and effect?**

    A so

    B walk

    C that

CHAPTER 8 SUMMARY

A **cause** is the reason why something happens.

An **effect** is the result.

Two ways to find the cause and effect are:
- **Think about the order of events**.
- **Look for key words**.

Cause and Effect

CHAPTER 8 REVIEW

ELA2R4 k

Read each story. Then, answer the questions.

Jean Watches the Door
A Cajun Folktale, Part 1

Jean's mom was going to shop.

"Jean," she said, "You're a teenager now. I have a task for you. I want you to take care of the house. Watch the door."

"Yes, Mama," Jean said.

Jean's mom left. She was gone a very long time.

Jean got worried. He wanted to look for her. But he had promised to watch the door.

So Jean took the door. He put it on his back while he went to look for his mother.

1 Why does Jean's mom ask him to watch the door?

   A She is leaving the house.

   B She is making dinner.

   C She is going to sleep.

2 What causes Jean to get worried?

   A His door is missing.

   B His house is cold.

   C His mom is not home.

Chapter 8

3 Jean's mom asks him to watch the door. He does not understand what she means. What does this cause Jean to do?

A Take care of the house.

B Take the door.

C Take a nap.

Jean and the Robbers
A Cajun Folktale, Part 2

Jean was looking for his mom. He saw a gang of robbers coming down the road.

Jean was scared. He tried to hide. He carried his door up a tree. But the robbers stood beneath the tree!

They sat down to count their money. One robber said to the rest, "This money is for you. And, this money is for you."

"And the rest is for me," Jean cried.

"Who said that?" said a robber. He looked all around but did not see Jean in the tree.

Jean was so scared he began to shake. He shook so hard he dropped the door.

"The tree is throwing doors at us!" yelled one of the robbers. They were so scared that they ran away.

Jean climbed down and took his door home. His mom was home. She was very confused.

4 Seeing the robbers causes Jean to

A get in a fight.

B hide in a tree.

C go shopping.

Cause and Effect

5 Why does Jean drop his door?

  A He sees his mom.

  B He has too much money.

  C He is shaking with fear.

6 Why is Jean's mom confused?

  A She wonders why he is carrying a door.

  B She wonders what time it is.

  C She wonders where her house is.

Chapter 9
Graphics

This chapter addresses the following Georgia grade 2 reading standard:

| ELA2R4 | g. Interprets information from illustrations, diagrams, charts, graphs, and graphic organizers. |

WHAT ARE GRAPHICS?

On a piece of paper, write this:

> Molly is a long, green snake. She likes to wear funny hats.

Think about what Molly looks like. Now, draw a snake that looks like Molly.

You just made a graphic! **Graphics** are pictures. They help you see what a passage is about.

A history book tells about people and places. Graphics can show you what they look like.

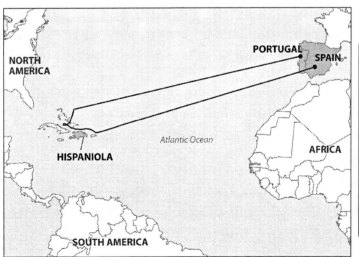

Christopher Columbus's Route to the Americas

Abraham Lincoln

115

Graphics

Some stories might have charts to help you understand. Look at this example.

Opal and her mom went shopping. They bought shirts and pants. Here is a chart of what they bought.

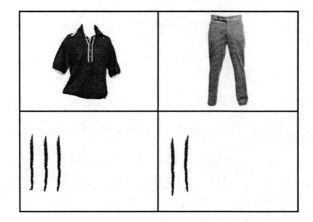

This chapter will look at all kinds of graphics.

ILLUSTRATIONS

Many stories come with pictures. They show you what a person looks like. Or, they can show what is happening in the story.

They *illustrate* what is going on. That is why they are called **illustrations**.

Let's look at an example.

George Washington

George Washington was an honest person. But, many people tell a legend about him. It is called a legend because it is not true.

This is how the story goes. When George was a little boy, he got a new ax. He was very happy with his ax. He cut down a cherry tree.

His dad saw the tree. He asked George about the tree. George said, "I cannot tell a lie. I cut it with my ax." His dad was happy that George told the truth.

Chapter 9

The story may not be true, but it is a good one! It was made up to show what kind of person George was. He was very honest.

Which picture BEST illustrates this story?

A

B

C

Take a close look at the pictures. Which one goes along with the story? The second picture shows a little boy chopping down a tree. That is the best picture to choose.

Did you pick that one?

Graphics

Activity: Draw It!

Read this short story. Then, draw three pictures to illustrate parts of the story. Have a friend or parent guess which picture goes with each part of the story.

Sammy and the Buried Treasure

Sammy wants to be a pirate. He wants to hunt for buried treasure. He wakes up one day and finds a piece of paper by his bed.

He looks at it closely. It has pictures on it. They look like clues. Sammy cannot figure it out.

In the bottom corner of the paper, there is a big X. Sammy knows what that means. X marks the spot! This must be a treasure map.

Sammy hops out of bed and puts on his pirate hat. He also wears his lucky eye patch. He's going to find a treasure.

He follows the map. It leads him around the house. He goes through the kitchen. He goes down to the basement. He follows the map outside. It leads him to his backyard.

"Surprise!" Sammy hears people yell. It is his friends and family. It is Sammy's birthday! The map led him to his party. What a fun way to celebrate!

Chapter 9

Practice 1: Illustrations
ELA2R4 g

Shamrock

The shamrock is a symbol of Ireland. A symbol reminds us of a place or thing. Think about the US flag. It is a symbol of the United States.

A shamrock is a kind of clover. It has three leaves. Some clovers have four leaves. We call this kind a "four-leaf clover." Some people think they bring good luck.

The Irish use shamrocks in many ways. You can see them on clothes. You see them in decorations. They were even used to make medicine.

St. Patrick's Day is an Irish holiday. It happens in March. On this day, people wear green. Many people wear shamrocks too.

1 What picture would BEST go along with this story?

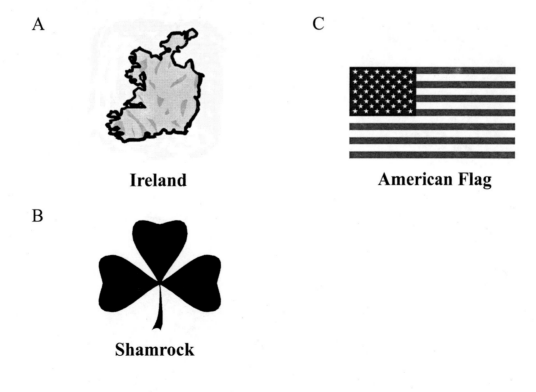

Graphics

2 Pretend you took a photo of a shamrock. What color would the leaves be?

A green

B orange

C blue

3 How many leaves do "lucky" clovers have?

A two

B three

C four

4 Draw a picture of someone dressed up for St. Patrick's Day.

Chapter 9

CHARTS

A **chart** helps to put things in order. It is a way to look at how many things there are. It can help you see what happens over time. It can compare two or more things.

PIE CHARTS

A **pie chart** is a way to show parts of a whole. It can tell you, "How many?"

Amanda asked ten friends what state they were born in. The whole pie is all of her ten friends. Each piece is a part of the whole group. It shows what they said.

Where Were Amanda's Friends Born?

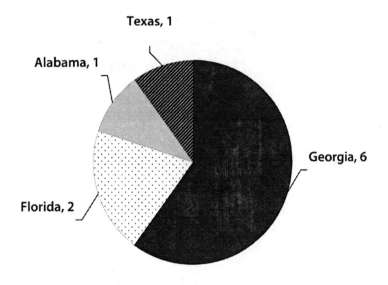

Where were MOST of Amanda's friends born?

A Florida

B Texas

C Georgia

Did you pick C? You are right! You can tell because the slice that shows Georgia is the biggest. Six of her friends were born in Georgia. That is more than were born in any other state.

Graphics

LINE CHARTS

A **line chart** can show things over time. You might hear them called line graphs. This one is from a little restaurant called Nell's Home Cooking. It shows how many people ate at Nell's every day last week.

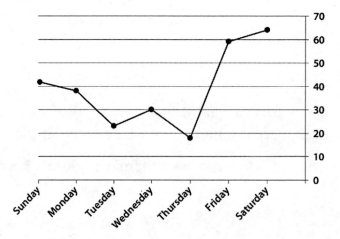

Practice 2: Charts

ELA2R4 g

Look at the chart about Nell's Home Cooking. Then, answer the questions.

1. On which day did the MOST people eat at Nell's?

   A Friday

   B Saturday

   C Sunday

2. On which day did the FEWEST people eat at Nell's?

   A Tuesday

   B Wednesday

   C Thursday

3. About how many people ate at Nell's on Monday?

   A 30

   B 38

   C 42

Chapter 9

Now, look at this pie chart. Then, answer the questions.

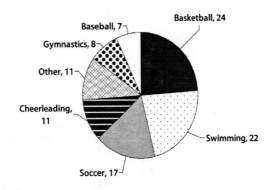

What Sports Kids Play
(out of 100 people)

* Other sports are football, extreme sports, hockey, tennis, and so on

4 What sport do MOST kids play?

A baseball

B cheerleading

C basketball

5 Martin plays hockey. Hockey is in the "Other" sports group. How many kids are in this group?

A 11

B 17

C 24

6 How many kids do gymnastics?

A 7

B 8

C 11

7 Which sport do 17 kids play?

A baseball

B football

C soccer

123

Graphics

DIAGRAMS

A **diagram** lets you see how a thing works. It shows the parts. It can let you see what is inside too. Say you get a new toy. You might have to put the pieces in the right places. A diagram shows you how the parts fit.

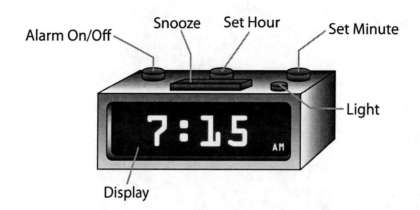

Practice 3: Diagrams

ELA2R4 g

Look at this diagram. It is a butterfly. Then, answer the questions.

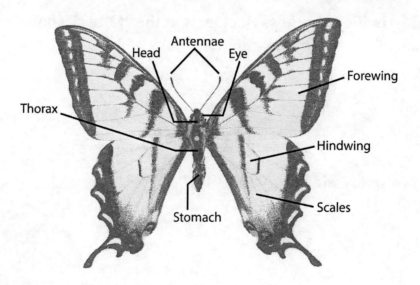

1   On a butterfly, where are the scales?

   A   the head

   B   the wings

   C   the thorax

Chapter 9

2 **What body part are the antennae connected to?**

A abdomen

B scales

C head

3 **What part of the body is between the head and the abdomen?**

A thorax

B hindwing

C eyes

CHAPTER 9 SUMMARY

Graphics are pictures. They help you see what the words say. These are the kinds of graphics:

- An **illustration** is a picture that goes with a story. It shows what something looks like.

- A **chart** helps to put things in order. A **pie chart** is a way to show parts of a whole. A **line chart** can show things over time.

- A **diagram** lets you see how a thing works. It shows the parts of something.

Graphics

CHAPTER 9 REVIEW

ELA2R4 g

Look at this chart. Then, answer the questions.

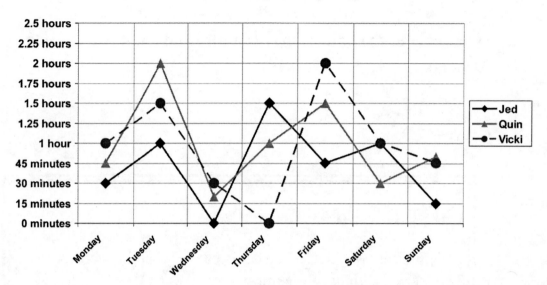

1. Two children each skipped a day of studying. Which child studied every day?

   A Jed

   B Quin

   C Vicki

2. On Thursday, who studied the MOST?

   A Jed

   B Quin

   C Vicki

3. On what day did Vicki study the MOST?

   A Tuesday

   B Wednesday

   C Friday

4 On Sunday, who studied the LEAST?

   A Jed

   B Quin

   C Vicki

Eye Doctor

Tina cannot see the board at school. Her eyes make it look blurry. So, she goes to the eye doctor.

She sits down in the big chair. The doctor looks at her eyes. He has her read the letters on a chart. He tells Tina that she needs glasses. He shows her a diagram of the eye. He tells Tina about each part.

He tells her the iris is the colored part of the eye. The pupil is the dark part in the middle.

The cornea is clear. It covers the iris and pupil. The lens sends pictures to the retina.

The optic nerve sends the pictures to the brain. Tina is learning a lot about her eyes.

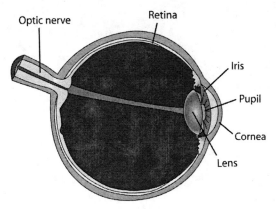

5 In the diagram, which part of the eye is covered by the iris and pupil?

   A cornea

   B lens

   C retina

Graphics

6 What part of the eye sends pictures to the brain?

A pupil

B iris

C optic nerve

7 What picture would BEST illustrate this story?

A

B

C

Chapter 9

Career Day

Today is Career Day at school. All the kids dress up. They show what they want to be when they grow up. It is fun to see what jobs everyone wants.

Gabe dresses up like a doctor. He wants to help people. Annie looks like a movie star. She wants to be famous one day. Hector is dressed like a firefighter.

Here is a chart of all the students in Mr. Johnson's class. It shows how they all dressed up.

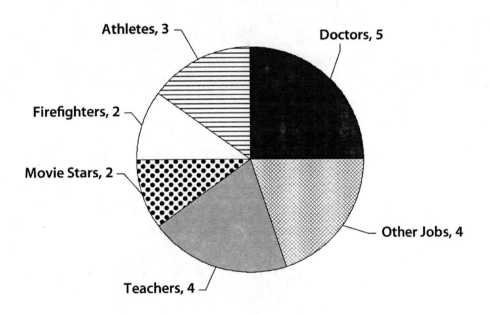

* Other jobs include police officers, lawyers, plumbers, zookeepers, principals, and so on.

8 In the story, who dresses like a movie star?

A Gabe

B Annie

C Hector

Graphics

9 In the chart, how many students dress up like teachers?

A 2

B 3

C 4

10 Molly dresses up like a lawyer. She fits in the Other Jobs group. How many kids are in that group?

A 4

B 5

C 6

11 How many MORE doctors are there than firefighters?

A 1

B 2

C 3

Chapter 10
Graphic Organizers

This chapter addresses the following Georgia grade 2 reading standard:

| ELA2R4 | g. Interprets information from illustrations, diagrams, charts, graphs, and graphic organizers. |

You read about graphics in the last chapter. There are many kinds. This chapter is about one more kind.

This kind of graphic helps organize ideas. That's why they are called **graphic organizers**. This chapter will show you a few kinds. Your teacher can show you others.

SORTING

Some graphic organizers help **sort** things. They can show what items or ideas go together. They can show how those items or ideas are the same.

131

Graphic Organizers

VENN DIAGRAM

One is called the **Venn diagram**. It helps you see how two objects are the same and different. It has two circles.

In one circle, you see facts about the first thing. The other circle has facts about the second thing.

In the middle, the circles overlap. This area has facts about both things.

Look at this Venn diagram. It shows how cats and birds are the same. It also shows how they are different.

Chapter 10

BASKETS

Items can also be sorted into groups. Each group can go in a **basket**. It's not a real basket. It's a picture of a basket. Here is an example.

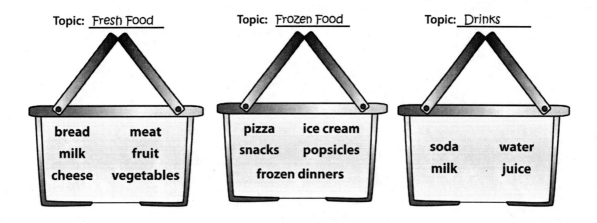

Practice 1: Sorting
ELA2R4 g

Look back at the baskets. See what they can tell you about things in a grocery store.

1 What is there MOST of in the grocery store?

   A fresh foods

   B frozen foods

   C drinks

2 Which item is in two baskets?

   A bread

   B milk

   C snacks

Graphic Organizers

3 What is another good way you can sort the food in a grocery store?

A

B

C

4 Look at the facts in the Fact Bank. Some of them are about popsicles. Some are about ice cream. Some are about both. Put the facts in the right place.

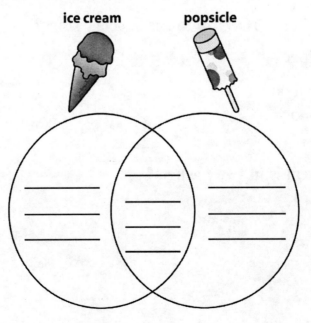

Chapter 10

Fact Bank	
needs a spoon	cold
dessert	harder
mostly on a stick	will melt
different flavors	softer
can add toppings	doesn't need a spoon

TIME ORDER

Graphic organizers can put events in order. They can show **time order**. That means they tell you when things happen.

TIMELINE

Look at this example. It is a **timeline**. It shows what happens first, second, third, and so on.

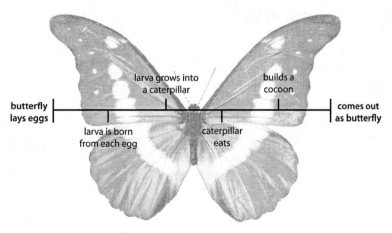

Now, see if you can answer some questions.

What happens NEXT after a caterpillar eats?

A It helps a larva hatch out of an egg.

B It makes a cocoon around itself.

C It becomes a pretty butterfly.

Graphic Organizers

Did you pick B? You are right! First, the caterpillar eats. Then, it makes its cocoon. The timeline shows you this.

Before a larva can be born, what must happen?

A A caterpillar must come out of a cocoon.

B A caterpillar needs to eat a lot of food.

C A butterfly has to lay some eggs.

The clue in this question is the word <u>before</u>. This means you have to look back. What happens before the larva hatches? That's right! The butterfly has to lay eggs.

STORY TRAIN

A **story train** shows the order of a story. Look at this example.

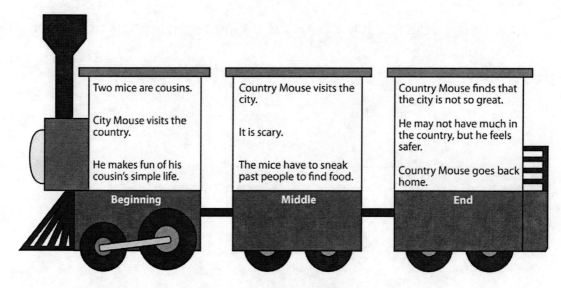

Where are the mice at the start of the story?

A in the city

B in the country

C on a train

Did you pick B? That's right! At the start, city mouse comes for a visit. He stays with his cousin in the country.

Chapter 10

Practice 2: Time Order
ELA2R4 g

Look back at the story train about the city mouse and the country mouse. Now, answer the questions about it.

1. Where does the middle of the story take place?

    A in the city

    B in the country

    C on a train

2. At the end, where are the mice?

    A Both mice are in the country.

    B They are in the city.

    C One is in the city, and one is in the country.

3. How many times does Country Mouse go to the city?

    A never

    B one time

    C two times

4. Why does Country Mouse not like the city?

    A It is scary.

    B There is no food.

    C He does not like City Mouse.

Graphic Organizers

Look at this timeline. Then, answer the questions.

Lori's brother Lance is in high school. He won the science fair this year! Lori asked him how he did it. He made this timeline.

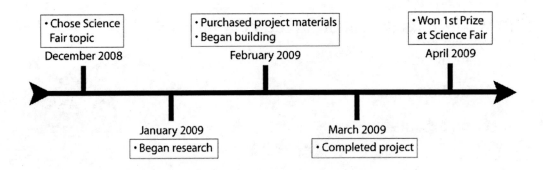

5 How many months did it take Lance to build his project?

A one month

B three months

C six months

6 What did Lance do just before he started to build?

A He picked a topic.

B He did some research.

C He finished the project.

7 Which of these things did Lance MOST LIKELY do in February?

A He wrote down ideas for different projects he could do.

B He invited his family to come to the science fair.

C He asked his parents for some money.

Chapter 10

> ## CHAPTER 10 SUMMARY
>
> A **graphic organizer** helps you with ideas.
>
> - It can help **sort** items and ideas. **Venn diagrams** are good for sorting. **Baskets** are also helpful.
> - It can show **time order**. A **timeline** and a **story train** show when events happen.

CHAPTER 10 REVIEW

ELA2R4 g

Look at each graphic organizer. Decide what it shows you. Then, answer the questions.

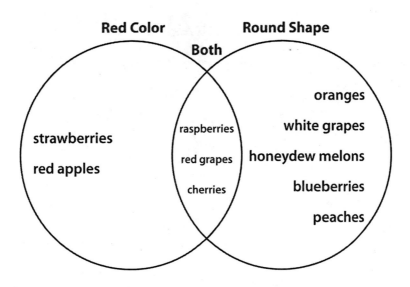

Kinds of Fruit

1. What does this Venn diagram show you?

    A which fruits are red or round or both

    B which fruits are sweet or tangy or both

    C which fruits are round or have pits or both

139

Graphic Organizers

2 Which kinds of fruits are there MOST of?

  A ones that are red but not round

  B ones that are both red and round

  C ones that are round but not red

3 Which of these fruits is both red and round?

  A blueberries

  B raspberries

  C strawberries

4 Which fruit is in two groups?

  A grapes

  B oranges

  C strawberries

Chapter 10

Costumes for Halloween

Group 1: Jobs People Have
- doctor
- nurse
- athlete
- police officer
- firefighter

Group 2: _____
- Batman
- The Incredibles
- Spider-Man
- Storm
- Superman

Group 3: Story Characters
- angel
- clown
- pirate
- princess
- wizard

5 What should Group 2 be called?

A Real People

B Superheroes

C Circus Characters

6 Jackie wants to dress up like a teacher. Which group would her costume be in?

A group 1

B group 2

C group 3

7 What is one thing in Group 1 that a kid can already do?

A be a doctor

B be an athlete

C be a firefighter

8 Which of these costumes would BEST fit in Group 2?

A Dora the Explorer

B Wonder Woman

C Clifford the Big Red Dog

Graphic Organizers

Jack and the Beanstalk

9 When does Jack's mom get mad?

   A when Jack takes the cow away

   B when Jack brings home only a few beans

   C when Jack chops down the big stalk that led to riches

10 Jack climbs the big stalk after

   A planting the magic beans.

   B the giant gets mad at him.

   C he escapes from the giant.

11 Who are the characters you see at the end of the story?

   A Jack, his mom, and their cow

   B Jack and the giant

   C Jack and his mom

Chapter 10

12 **Say that you want to add a piece of the story. Where should you MOST LIKELY put this?**

> The giant sees Jack coming up the stalk.

A at the start

B in the middle

C at the end

Graphic Organizers

Chapter 11
Learning Words

This chapter addresses the following Georgia grade 2 reading standards:

ELA2R3	a. Reads a variety of texts and uses new words in oral and written language (NOT TESTED).
	b. Recognizes grade appropriate words with multiple meanings.
	d. Determines the meaning of unknown words on the basis of context.
ELA2R4	q. Uses dictionary, thesaurus, and glossary skills to determine word meanings. (NOT TESTED)

It is great to learn new words. Some are easy to learn. Some are not so easy. You know what <u>win</u> means, right? Do you know what <u>compete</u> means? Read on to find out.

CONTEXT CLUES

When you visit a new place, how do you act? Let's pretend you ate at a fancy place to eat. Would you do whatever you wanted? Or would you wait to see what other people do?

You would look at how other people acted. You might see how they order their food. You could see how they use their knife and fork. You would pay attention to the things around you.

Words are the same way. When you see a word you do not know, look at the words around it. **Context** means the things around a word.

Context clues give you hints about the meaning of a new word. Context clues come from the words around the new word.

Learning Words

Look at this example:

> It is fun to compete.

Look at the word compete. You may not know what this word means. Looking at it by itself does not tell you much about the meaning of the word.

Field trips are fun. Parties are fun. Games are fun. Do they all mean the same thing as compete? It's hard to tell what compete means.

Now, try reading this. This time, there are context clues.

> We like to play sports. We all play fair. Trying to win is fun. It is fun to compete.

The words around the word compete are context clues. Can you figure out what compete means using context clues?

Look at the words around compete to figure it out. Based on these clues, we can guess that the word compete means "try to win."

When you are unsure about a word, look at the words around it. Now, you know a little more about context clues. Let's practice.

Chapter 11

Practice 1: Context Clues
ELA2R3 d

Read the story. Then, answer the questions.

Wake Up!

Kendra is trying to watch a movie. But, she is so <u>weary</u>. She keeps falling asleep!

The movie made her laugh at first. The story is <u>amusing</u>. She just cannot stay awake.

She is happy that her cousin let her <u>borrow</u> the movie. She has to give it back tomorrow. So, she wants to finish watching it.

"Maybe I should <u>pause</u> it. Then, I'll do some jumping jacks to wake up," Kendra thinks.

1 Which word means the same as the word <u>weary</u>?

A lively

B tired

C happy

2 Which word means the same as the word <u>amusing</u>?

A funny

B happy

C excited

3 In this story, the word <u>borrow</u> means

A stop thinking about.

B keep watching.

C have for a short time.

Learning Words

4 In this story, what does the word <u>pause</u> mean?

A an animal's feet

B take a nap

C stop for a moment

SAME WORDS, DIFFERENT MEANINGS

Some words have **multiple meanings**. This means that one word can have more than one meaning. Context clues can help with this kind of word too. Look at what is around the word.

Here is an example:

> Brett is a <u>serious</u> person. He does not like jokes.

Do you know what <u>serious</u> means? Look at the context, and you can guess that it means "not funny."

But, <u>serious</u> has another meaning too. Look at the next sentence:

> The Olympic Games are for <u>serious</u> athletes only.

You can see that this use of <u>serious</u> does not mean "not funny." It means "very focused." The context of the word is different.

It will take time to learn words with more than one meaning. Just remember to look at the words around them to find what they mean.

Chapter 11

Practice 2: Words with Multiple Meanings
ELA2R3 b

Melissa

Melissa likes to be loud. Her voice is <u>piercing</u>. She yells and screams just for fun. Mom reminds her to speak in a <u>low</u> voice. Melissa does not like to be quiet.

One day, Melissa was in her room. She saw a <u>mouse</u>. It scared her. She shouted, "MOM! DAD!" But, no one came.

She ran downstairs. She asked them why they did not come to help her.

Dad said, "We thought you were just yelling for fun. Now you know why we ask you not to yell all the time."

1 In this story, what does the word <u>piercing</u> mean?

   A bright

   B noisy

   C spiky

2 In this story, what does the word <u>low</u> mean?

   A sad

   B short

   C quiet

Learning Words

3 In this story, what does the word <u>mouse</u> mean?

   A a furry rodent

   B a part of a computer

   C a shy person

LOOK IT UP!

There is a good way to learn about a word. How? Look it up!

When you see a new word, look up what it means. Here are some tools you can use to look up a word.

DICTIONARY

A **dictionary** shows what words mean. Words are in ABC order. That makes them easy to find.

The top of each page tells you the first word on that page. It also tells you the last word. You just need to know where the word fits that you are looking up.

To look up a word, use the first letter. This means the word <u>ant</u> comes before the word <u>bat</u>. A comes before B.

If the first letter is the same, use the second letter, and so on. This means that <u>act</u> comes before <u>ant</u>. And, <u>art</u> comes after <u>ant</u>. See how it works? Now, you try it.

If you want to look up the word <u>rest</u>, which page would you look on? Here are the first and last words at the top of the page.

  Which page would have <u>rest</u> on it?

   A rat – rent

   B react – roost

   C treat – trust

Chapter 11

Did you pick answer B? You're right! We know it can't be C, because rest would not be on a page of words that start with the letter T. Why is answer A wrong? Rest comes after rent, which is the last word on that page. So, it can't be on that page. The first two letters are the same (R and E), but the third letter, S in rest, comes after N in rent.

When you find a word, you will see what it means. We can look up the word bat in a dictionary. This is what it says:

> **bat**
>
> **1.** a flying animal
>
> **2.** a stick used for baseball
>
> **3.** to hit

As you can see, bat can mean more than one thing. It's one of those words we talked about. It has multiple meanings.

You could…

hear a bat flying in the sky.   swing at a fastball with a bat.   bat at a piñata.

What about the word collapse?

Read this sentence:

> Mom said, "Jim, collapse the folding chair. It is in the way."

Learning Words

Look up the word collapse. You can find it in a dictionary. Here is what you will likely find:

> **collapse**
> 1. to fall down
> 2. to fold
> 3. to break

Knocking the chair over will not help. So, number **1** is not right.

Jim is probably not strong enough to break a folding chair, so number **3** is not right.

If Jim folds the chair, that might make more space. So, number **2** is the right meaning.

Now we see what collapse means.

GLOSSARY

A **glossary** shows what words mean too. It is also in ABC order. But, it is shorter. You can find it at the end of some books. It lists the words used in that one book.

Say you finished a book. It was all about video games. One part said that people who program make video games. You want to see what the word program means.

In the glossary, you see this:

> **online game** – a game played on the Web
> **program** – to instruct a computer
> **racing game** – a game based on racing

Can you see what program means in this book? Program can mean many other things. It can mean "a TV show." But, in a book about video games, it means one thing. It means "to tell a computer what to do."

Chapter 11

THESAURUS

There is one other place to look up a word. A **thesaurus** shows words that mean almost the same thing.

Here is an example:

> **pretty** – attractive, beautiful, cute, good-looking

As you can see, a thesaurus does not explain what a word means. It just shows words that mean close to the same thing.

Activity: Look It Up!

Read this passage. Do you know all the words? Look up words that are new to you. Write down what they mean on your own paper.

Andy and Daisy
adapted from fable by Aesop

Andy the Ant went to the bank of a river to quench his thirst. Andy was hauled away by the rush of the stream. He could not get out of the water.

"Help!" shouted Andy.

Daisy the Dove plucked a leaf and let it fall into the water. Andy scrambled onto it and floated to the bank. He was grateful to Daisy.

That night, a man saw Daisy asleep in her tree. He wanted to snag her with a net.

Andy the Ant bit the man's big toe. The man yelped in surprise.

Daisy jolted awake when she heard the man shout. She saw that he had a net. She flew away. She thanked Andy.

Learning Words

> ### CHAPTER 11 SUMMARY
>
> **Context** means words around a new word. Context clues give you hints about the meaning of a new word.
>
> Some words have **multiple meanings**. Look at the context to find their meanings.
>
> A **dictionary** shows what words mean. A **glossary** lists words that are used in one book. A **thesaurus** shows words that mean close to the same thing.

CHAPTER 11 REVIEW

ELA2R3 b & d

Read each passage. Then, answer the questions.

Moving Out

Will's big sister is moving out. She is <u>packing</u> her bags in her car. She is going away to college.

Will is sad that she is leaving. He tells her he feels <u>gloomy</u>. She says she is sad too.

But, Will is <u>glad</u> about one thing. He gets to have her old room. It has a big window.

Will hugs his sister goodbye. She will visit him soon. He goes up to his new room. He <u>peers</u> out the window. He sees her car driving away.

1. In this story, the word <u>packing</u> means

   A driving.

   B stealing.

   C putting.

Chapter 11

2 In this story, what does the word <u>gloomy</u> mean?

A cheerful

B sad

C scared

3 Which word means the same as the word <u>glad</u>?

A pleased

B unsure

C cruel

4 **In this story, the word <u>peers</u> means**

A looks.

B friends.

C jumps.

Wind Power

Power makes things work. Many things <u>operate</u> because of power. There are a lot of ways to make power.

Wind Farm

Some places use water for power. Some places burn trash for power. That is true for many places in Georgia. This can be very dirty. It can make the air smell <u>dreadful</u>.

One way to make power is to use wind farms. A wind farm uses <u>breezes</u> to make power. It is very clean.

Why not use wind power in all places? Some areas don't have enough wind. Georgia is just not <u>windy</u> enough!

155

Learning Words

5 In this passage, what does the word <u>operate</u> mean?

   A surgery

   B work

   C manage

6 In this passage, the word <u>dreadful</u> means

   A awful.

   B dreamy.

   C weird.

7 In this passage, the word <u>breezes</u> means

   A pieces of wood.

   B buckets of water.

   C gusts of wind.

8 In this passage, the word <u>windy</u> means

   A full of wind.

   B full of turns.

   C full of power.

Chapter 12
Word Roots

This chapter addresses the following Georgia grade 2 reading standard:

| ELA2R4 | p. Uses word parts to determine meanings. |

Many things have roots. Trees have roots. Flowers have roots. Even your teeth have roots!

Words have roots too. Read on to find out about word roots and how they work.

ROOTS

A **root** is the main part of a word. Often, a word is nothing but a root. The word <u>dance</u> is a root.

Here is another word that is a root:

friend = a person you know and like

> **Example:** Anuk is my best friend.

Other word parts can be added to a root. They can be added to the start and the end. The added parts are not words. But, they can change a root into a new word.

You can read more about other word parts in chapter 13.

Here is the root <u>friend</u> with some word parts added. The main word part is the root. New parts make new words. See how each new word is like the root word?

-ly is a word part that means <u>like</u>

friendly = <u>like</u> a friend

> **Example:** Cathy's cat is very <u>friendly</u>. He purrs and plays with me.

Word Roots

un- is a word part that means <u>not</u>

unfriendly = <u>not</u> like a friend

> **Example:** The new kid down the street won't talk to us. He's being <u>unfriendly</u>.

-ship is a word part that means <u>state of</u>

friendship = the <u>state of</u> being friends

> **Example:** Remy and Molly have a great <u>friendship</u>.

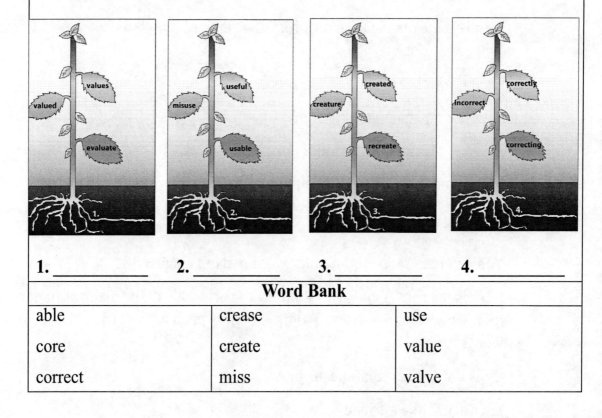

Activity: Roots

Look at each plant. The leaves have words on them. These words have the same root. Can you find out which root it is?

Use the word bank to choose which root word goes with each plant. Some words in the word bank will not be used. Write the word on the root.

1. _____ 2. _____ 3. _____ 4. _____

Word Bank		
able	crease	use
core	create	value
correct	miss	valve

158

Chapter 12

Practice 1: Roots
ELA2R4 p

Read the story. Then, answer the questions.

The Zoo

Bucky and I are at the <u>zoo</u>. We see animals all over the place. Some are in cages. Some are in deep pools of water. Some have big areas to roam in.

We meet a <u>zookeeper</u>. She has a fun job. She takes care of the elephants. She feeds them every day. Sometimes, she wishes she could let them run free.

She says she is going to college. She is studying to become a scientist. She wants to study animals. She says the study of animals is called <u>zoology</u>.

1. In this story, the word <u>zoo</u> means

   A a deep pool of water.

   B a place to see animals.

   C a big area to roam in.

2. What is the <u>zookeeper</u>'s job?

   A wishing she could free the elephants

   B building cages for the elephants

   C taking care of the elephants

Word Roots

3 In this story, what does the word <u>zoology</u> mean?

A the study of animals

B a kind of elephant

C the study of scientists

Now, answer a few more questions.

4 Which of these words is a root word?

A preview

B viewing

C view

5 What is the root word for both <u>happiness</u> and <u>unhappy</u>?

A happ

B happy

C happen

6 Which of these words is a root word?

A walker

B walk

C walking

7 Which word is made from the root word <u>music</u>?

A musical

B muscle

C mustard

Chapter 12

COMPOUND WORDS

A **compound word** is a word made of two root words.

Houseboat is a compound word. It is made of two words: house and boat. It means "a boat that people live in like a house." Of course!

Can you figure out what these compound words mean?

armchair	hilltop
backspin	watchdog
earring	

Got it? Take a look at what they mean:

armchair	a chair that also supports a person's arms
backspin	the way a ball spins one way while flying another
earring	a ring that goes in a person's ear
hilltop	the top of a hill
watchdog	a dog that watches to make sure people are safe

Watchdog

Armchair

161

Word Roots

Not all compound words are this easy. Try this activity!

Activity: Compound Words

Each word below is split up into parts. Draw a picture for each part. Then add the parts to make the compound word. Use the first one as an example.

+ =	snow + shoe = <u>snowshoe</u>
+ =	fire + fly = _____
+ =	cross + walk _____
+ =	saw + horse = _____
+ =	bed + time = _____

Chapter 12

Now, take a look at the pictures below. Find out what compound word the pictures make. The first one is done for you.

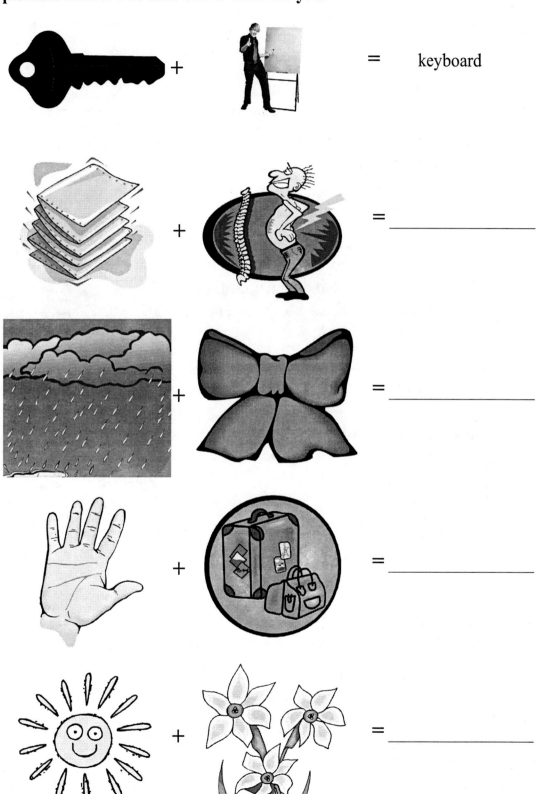

Word Roots

Practice 2: Compound Words

ELA2R4 p

Read the story. Then, answer the questions.

Little Brother

Alex is my stepbrother. His mom married my dad. We have fun.

He is younger than me. He always wants to play. Yesterday, I gave him a piggyback ride. I carried him on my back for a long time.

I carried him from the house. I ran to the mailbox. Then, I put him down. Next, we had a race uphill to the porch. We wiped our feet on the doormat and went inside.

Alex is a good stepbrother. I don't think of him as my stepbrother though. He just seems like a brother to me.

1 Which of these words is a compound word?

A married

B stepbrother

C younger

2 What is a piggyback ride?

A Two people race from a house to a mailbox.

B A kid likes having fun with a sibling.

C One person carries another on his back.

Chapter 12

Read this sentence from the passage.

> Next, we had a race uphill to the porch.

3 Which word has two parts?

A next

B uphill

C porch

4 The opposite of <u>uphill</u> is

A upgrade.

B quickly.

C downhill.

5 How many word parts are in the word <u>doormat</u>?

A 1

B 2

C 3

CHAPTER 12 SUMMARY

Words are made of parts.

A **root** is the main part of a word.

A **compound word** is a word made of two words.

Word Roots

CHAPTER 12 REVIEW

ELA2R4 p

Read each story. Then, answer the questions.

Jenna's Typewriter

Jenna likes to write. She writes recipes. She writes poems. Her friends like to read her ghost stories.

Many people write in notebooks. Or, they type. Jenna likes to type. She types on an old <u>typewriter</u>.

"What's a typewriter?" I ask.

She shows me. It looks like a <u>keyboard</u>. But, it has other parts too. They make a lot of noise when she types.

Jenna likes the <u>noisy</u> machine. She likes having to turn dials if she pushes a wrong key. This makes her care more about what she writes.

1 Which of these words in the story is a compound word?

   A recipes

   B notebooks

   C machine

2 In this story, the word <u>noisy</u> means

   A having other parts.

   B making a lot of noise.

   C looking like a computer.

3 In this story, the word <u>key</u> means

   A a small button on a machine.

   B an item that can lock a door.

   C a guide to reading a map.

4 How many word roots are in the word <u>keyboard</u>?

   A 1

   B 2

   C 3

5 How many word parts are in the word <u>typewriter</u>?

   A 1

   B 2

   C 3

How Real is *Rock Band*?

Many people play *Rock Band*. It is a video game. Players can pretend to play music. But, is playing *Rock Band* like <u>playing</u> real music?

Eve, Bo, and Mark play *Rock Band* together. Eve plays the drums. She uses real sticks. They are called <u>drumsticks</u>. She uses them to hit the drums. Some songs are very fast. *Rock Band*'s drums seem almost real.

Bo likes to play guitar. The guitar is not very real. It has no strings. It just has buttons. Still, it takes practice. Bo wants to learn to play real guitar someday.

Word Roots

Mark is the band's <u>singer</u>. He sings into a real microphone. In the game, the singing is very real.

As you can see, *Rock Band* has some parts that are real. It is a good way to start learning how to be a <u>musician</u>.

6 What is the root word of the word <u>**playing**</u>?

A play

B plain

C player

7 How many root words are in the word <u>**drumsticks**</u>?

A 1

B 2

C 3

8 What is the root word of the word <u>**singer**</u>?

A sing

B singe

C ger

9 Which word is a compound word?

A game

B someday

C singing

10 In this story, the word <u>**musician**</u> means

A someone who plays games.

B someone who has friends.

C someone who plays music.

Chapter 13
Other Word Parts

This chapter addresses the following Georgia grade 2 reading standard:

| ELA2R4 | p. Uses word parts to determine meanings. |

In chapter 12, you can read about roots. Roots are word parts. You can see how a word part changes a root word into a new word!

There are other **word parts**. They all get added on to roots. They can tell you how many things there are. Or, they can tell you when something happens.

Read on for more about each of these.

THE S RULE

HOW MANY ARE THERE?

Look at these two words: neighbor and neighbors.

What is the difference? It's the s at the end of the word. This is **the s rule**: to make a word mean "more than one," add an s. Some words do not use this rule. But, most words do.

A neighbor is just one.

Neighbor means "one neighbor."

Neighbors means "more than one neighbor."

It could be two neighbors.

It could be a crowd of neighbors!

Other Word Parts

Here are some other words that use the s rule:

One thing	More than one thing
banana	bananas
feather	feathers
knight	knights
porcupine	porcupines

Chapter 13

Some words use <u>es</u> instead of <u>s</u>. Here are a few:

One thing		More than one thing	
brush		brushes	
dress		dresses	
mailbox		mailboxes	
watch		watches	

Practice 1: The <u>s</u> Rule
ELA2R4 p

Read the story. Then, answer the questions.

Playing Cards with the Boys

Carla is about to play cards with her brothers. Her oldest brother, Gary, will teach them all a game. He knows many games.

At first, Carla does not know how to play. She does not win the first round. Her brother Tom has better cards.

She does not win the second round either. She doesn't win any of the first ten rounds!

Other Word Parts

Her brothers make fun of her. She laughs. She says she will win the next round. She makes a wish to win.

1. What word means "more than one card?"

   A card

   B cards

   C cardes

2. Which of these words means more than one?

   A game

   B second

   C rounds

3. What word means "more than one brother"?

   A brotheres

   B brothers

   C brother

4. If Carla made more than one wish, she would make

   A wishs.

   B wishes.

   C washes.

Chapter 13

WORDS THAT DO NOT USE THE S RULE

The s rule is a simple rule. But, some words are different. Some words do not use this rule. They use another word. The word teeth is one. It means "more than one tooth."

One tooth: That tooth is very loose.

More than one tooth: Ice cream makes my teeth hurt.

Wrong: Ice cream makes my tooths hurt.

There are many words like this. They do not use the s rule. Here are some more words that do not use the s rule:

One thing	More than one thing
child	children (not childs)
man	men (not mans)
mouse	mice (not mouses)
sheep	sheep (not sheeps)

Some words do not use the s rule. You will have to learn these words one at a time.

Other Word Parts

Practice 2: Words That Do Not Use the s Rule
ELA2R4 p

Read each story. Then, answer the questions.

Learning about Deer

We saw a <u>deer</u> at the canyon. It was eating berries. It had big antlers.

When we got home, I wanted to learn more. I looked up deer on the computer. I learned many facts about <u>deer</u>. I read how they live and eat. I saw how baby deer look!

1 In this sentence, how many things does the word <u>deer</u> mean?

> We saw a <u>deer</u> at the canyon.

A 1

B more than 1

C There is no way to know.

2 In this sentence, how many things does the word <u>deer</u> mean?

> I learned many facts about <u>deer</u>.

A 1

B more than 1

C There is no way to know.

Running in the Field

I ran through the field. I ran without my shoes on. The cool grass felt good on both my _____.

When I finished running, I looked down. There was grass all over my right _____. There was grass all over my left one too.

Chapter 13

3 Which word should fill in the blank in this sentence?

| The cool grass felt good on my _____. |

A feets

B feet

C foot

4 Which word should fill in the blank in this sentence?

| There was grass all over my right _____. |

A foot

B feet

C foots

OTHER WORD ENDINGS

We just learned the s rule. An s is an ending. An **ending** is a type of word part. Can you guess where it goes? It goes at the END of a word. This makes a new word.

HOW DO THEY COMPARE?

There are three more kinds of endings. These endings are er, est, and ly. They are added to words that describe things.

THE ER ENDING

The first kind helps you answer which is MORE. It can help with questions like these:

- Which day was sunnier?
- Is Lisa's hair longer than Lara's?
- Whose desk is cleaner?

175

Other Word Parts

THE EST ENDING

The second kind helps you answer which is the MOST. It can help with questions like these:

- Which day was the sunniest?
- Does Lisa have the longest hair of anyone in her family?
- Whose desk is the cleanest?

THE LY ENDING

The third kind tells you HOW something happens. You can add it to words like kind or year.

Kind is a root. It means "nice."

> **Example:** Buster is a kind dog.

Add ly to kind. Kindly means "acting nice." You use it to describe an action.

> **Example:** Buster kindly makes sure Ben is safe.

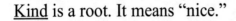

Year is a root. It means "365 days." It is the whole time between your last birthday and your next one!

> **Example:** We lived in Macon for one year.

Add ly to year. Yearly means "every year."

> **Example:** I went to the doctor for my yearly checkup.

Practice 3: How Do They Compare?
ELA2R4 p

Read the story. Then, answer the questions.

Jamie

Jamie feels fearless. Her mom and big sister have jumped into the lake. Now she wants to try it too.

She climbs up on the rock. She looks down. It looks like a long way down! It looks longer than it did before.

She tells herself not to be scared. She knows the water is deep enough. Her mom says it's safe to jump.

Jamie jumps. She feels like she is flying. Splash!

"You jumped fearlessly," says her mom.

"You are the bravest," says her sister.

1 In this story, the word fearless means

A courageous

B youthful

C pointless

2 What does longer mean?

A less long

B more long

C just as long

3 How many word parts are in the word fearlessly?

A 1

B 2

C 3

4 In this story, the word bravest means

A most jumpy

B most brave

C most little

Other Word Parts

WHEN DOES IT HAPPEN?

Here is one more kind of word ending. These word endings tell you WHEN an action happened. They are ing, ed, and s.

THE ING ENDING

If José plays soccer, we could say this:

> José is kicking the ball.

The ing on the end of kick is an ending. It makes a new word: kicking. It means that José is doing the kicking right now.

THE ED ENDING

What about this one?

> José kicked the ball.

The ed means José has already kicked the ball. He may have kicked the ball yesterday. He may have done it last week. But, he is not kicking it right now.

THE S ENDING

Here is one more:

> José kicks the ball.

Can you find the ending? Yes, s is the ending in kicks. It also makes a new word. It could mean he kicks right now. Or, it could mean he kicks all the time. It can mean that José kicks the ball in every game.

The Mighty s

An s is a very strong word part! It can change one thing into two things.

> cat
>
> cats

It can also show when an action happens.

> José kicks well every time!

178

Chapter 13

Activity: When Does It Happen?

Look at the pictures. Each has a word under it. It also has the time when it happens. This will help you choose what ending to put with the word.

There is a blank next to the picture. Write the word plus the right ending in the blank. Use words from the Word Bank. The first one is done for you.

1

washed

wash (yesterday)

2

pull (today)

3

sail (two months ago)

4

color (all the time)

5

wink (right now)

Word Bank

wash	pull	sail	color	wink
washes	pulls	sails	colors	winks
washing	pulling	sailing	coloring	winking
washed	pulled	sailed	colored	winked

Other Word Parts

Practice 4: When Does It Happen?
ELA2R4 p

Read the story. Then, answer the questions.

Volleyball

Marcy went to volleyball practice.

"We are going to practice <u>blocking</u> today," said Coach.

Coach showed the team how to block. She asked Marcy to send the ball over the net. Then, Coach jumped to knock the ball back across. She jumped very high.

"Wow!" said Marcy.

The team played a game. They all <u>blocked</u> each other. Soon, practice was over.

"Marcy <u>blocks</u> very well," Coach said to Marcy's parents.

1. How many word parts are in the word <u>blocking</u>?

   A 1

   B 2

   C 3

2. **The girls <u>blocked</u>.** When did this happen?

   A right now

   B tomorrow

   C in the past

Chapter 13

3 Which sentence uses the word <u>block</u> in the right way?

   A The player <u>blocks</u>.

   B The player <u>blocking</u>.

   C The player <u>block</u>.

MORE RULES ABOUT ENDINGS

Some words change spelling when you add an ending. If you just put the ending on, they look funny. For example, look at the word <u>try</u>. If you add the <u>ed</u> ending, it would be <u>tryed</u>. That's not right! It should be <u>tried</u>.

     Example: We always try to win. We lost, but we <u>tried</u> our best.

To add an <u>ed</u> to words that end in <u>y</u>, the <u>y</u> changes to an <u>i</u>. It's like this:

     Example: Nina is our spy. She <u>spied</u> on the other team.

Here is another rule.

To add <u>ed</u> or <u>ing</u> to a word like <u>drop</u>, the writer adds another <u>p</u>. It looks like this:

     Example: Don't drop the eggs. I <u>dropped</u> one yesterday. Look out! You are <u>dropping</u> it!

Why add another <u>p</u>? Some words have a vowel (<u>a</u>, <u>e</u>, <u>i</u>, <u>o</u>, <u>u</u>) and then one letter like <u>b</u>, <u>g</u>, <u>m</u>, <u>n</u>, <u>p</u>, or <u>t</u>. When that happens, the last letter needs to be doubled. Here are more examples:

     Examples: The class started to clap. We <u>clapped</u> as the band played.

                     Coach told us to jog around to warm up. We <u>jogged</u> around the track.

                     You can sit by the lake. Your friends are <u>sitting</u> there.

                     Ricky tried not to slip on the shiny floor. But soon, we were all <u>slipping</u> around on it!

Other Word Parts

CHAPTER 13 SUMMARY

Word parts are added to roots. This makes new words. Word parts help you answer questions.

The s rule: to make a word mean "more than one," add an s. For some words, you need to add es. Some words do not use this rule. They use a different word to show more than one.

An **ending** goes at the END of a word. This makes a new word.

- The **endings** er, est, and ly are added to words that describe.
- The **endings** ing, ed, and s tell you when an action happened.

Some words change **spelling** when they have an ending.

CHAPTER 13 REVIEW

ELA2R4 p

Read each story. Then, answer the questions.

Raptors

Have you <u>watched</u> *Jurassic Park*? It has animals called raptors. But, some things it <u>shows</u> about raptors aren't real.

In the movie, they are very big. They are <u>bigger</u> than grown-up people. In real life, they were not big. Most raptors were only as big as turkeys.

Speaking of birds, real raptors had feathers. They did not have skin like a <u>snake</u>.

The movie also makes raptors seem like the <u>smartest</u> animals. They were not all that smart in real life. But, they could <u>run</u> fast. The movie did show that!

1 Which sentence uses the word <u>watched</u> in the WRONG way?

   A I <u>watched</u> my uncle surf yesterday.

   B Marcus came over and <u>watched</u> basketball.

   C We will <u>watched</u> the dance team tomorrow.

2 Which sentence uses the word <u>shows</u> in the RIGHT way?

   A Dad <u>shows</u> the scar on his foot to Mike.

   B I'm going to <u>shows</u> Mom my report card.

   C She <u>shows</u> Patrick how to play golf last week.

Other Word Parts

3 How many word parts are in the word <u>bigger</u>?

   A 1

   B 2

   C 3

4 Which word means "more than one snake"?

   A snaks

   B snakes

   C snakkes

5 The word <u>smartest</u> means

   A less smart.

   B more smart.

   C most smart.

6 What is the RIGHT way to add <u>ing</u> to the word <u>run</u>?

   A runing

   B running *

   C runeing

Chapter 13

Alaska

Alaska is the largest state in the country. It is not near other states. But, it is still part of America.

It is really far north. That makes it colder than other states. So much snow falls in Alaska that schools don't close. Kids go to school in the snow.

Alaska has many places to live. It has big cities. It has small towns. This is just like Georgia and other states.

But, it also has towns that are far from other places. They do not have roads. You can only reach them by air. It helps to know someone who can fly a plane!

7 What does the word <u>largest</u> mean?

A less large

B more large

C most large

8 What is the root word of the word <u>really</u>?

A ally

B real

C reall

9 What does the word <u>colder</u> mean?

A not cold

B less cold

C more cold

Other Word Parts

10 What does the word <u>falls</u> mean in this sentence?

> So much snow <u>falls</u> in Alaska that schools don't close.

   A There is snow all the time in Alaska.

   B There used to be snow in Alaska.

   C There is hardly ever snow in Alaska.

11 Anchorage is a big city. It has the most people of any city in Alaska. How would you add the ending <u>est</u> to the word <u>big</u> to talk about this city?

   A bigest

   B biggest

   C bigiest

12 Which word means just one?

   A roads

   B towns

   C state

13 What is the right way to add <u>s</u> to the word <u>fly</u>?

   A flys

   B flyes

   C flies

Chapter 14
Word Meaning

This chapter addresses the following Georgia grade 2 reading standard(s):

ELA2R3	c. Recognizes and applies the appropriate usage of homophones, homographs, antonyms, and synonyms.

Here is a list of words you may not know:

considerate

narrow

which

minute

Do you know what these words mean? If not, you can find out. How? In chapter 11, you see that you can look them up in a dictionary. There are other ways too.

In this chapter, we will read about ways to find what words mean. And, we will find the meaning for each of the words above.

First, we can go over similar words.

Word Meaning

SYNONYMS

Synonyms are words that mean the same thing. They are similar words. This means two or more words can be alike. Or, they can be very close. It is simple. You know many words that mean the same thing.

Think about the word scary. Many words mean the same thing. Can you think of any? Here are a few:

  eerie

  frightful

  spooky

  terrifying

Now, what about the word considerate? It is in the list at the start of this chapter. What does considerate mean? We can figure it out.

> Kim is very considerate. She is kind and caring to everyone.

You can use the other words as context clues. To read more about context clues, see chapter 11.

The word considerate is like the words kind or caring. So, what if someone called you considerate? How would you feel? Is that a good thing or a bad thing?

Think about the other words that mean the same thing. Being kind and caring are good things. So, being considerate is good too!

Chapter 14

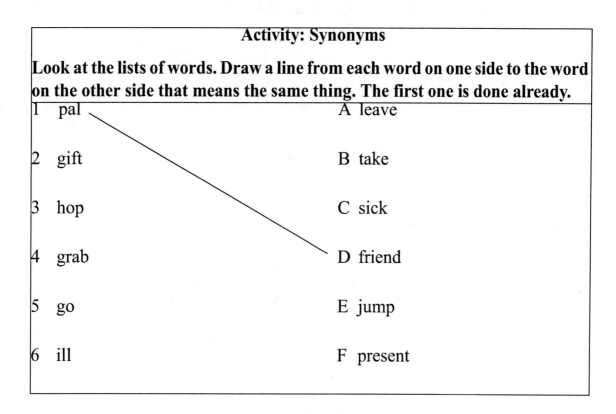

Activity: Synonyms

Look at the lists of words. Draw a line from each word on one side to the word on the other side that means the same thing. The first one is done already.

1 pal   A leave
2 gift   B take
3 hop   C sick
4 grab   D friend
5 go   E jump
6 ill   F present

Practice 1: Synonyms
ELA2R3 c

Read the passage. Then, answer the questions.

Nick's Big Move

Nick is moving away from Georgia. His dad got a job in another state. Nick is <u>worried</u> that no one will like him.

His mom and dad fill boxes with all of their things. Nick fills boxes too. They work until their backs <u>ache</u>! They put the boxes in a <u>giant</u> van.

They drive a long way to their new house. Finally, Dad says they are <u>close</u>. They come around a <u>bend</u> and see their new house. Nick <u>likes</u> it. He starts to feel excited about his new home!

Word Meaning

1. In this story, the word <u>worried</u> means

   A nervous.

   B excited.

   C tired.

2. Which of these words means the same thing as <u>ache</u>?

   A flop

   B hurt

   C bend

3. Which word means the same as <u>giant</u>?

   A small

   B happy

   C huge

4. In this story, the word <u>close</u> means the same as

   A lost.

   B near.

   C here.

5. In this story, the word <u>bend</u> means the same as which word?

   A building

   B storm

   C turn

6. In the last part of the story, which two words can mean the same thing?

   A <u>house</u> and <u>home</u>

   B <u>long</u> and <u>new</u>

   C <u>come</u> and <u>start</u>

Chapter 14

ANTONYMS

Antonyms are words that do not mean the same thing. They are opposite words.

Think about <u>black</u> and <u>white</u>. Are they the same? No, <u>black</u> and <u>white</u> mean opposite colors. <u>In</u> and <u>out</u> are opposite too.

Here are some others:

Opposite Words					
deep	summer	truth	nice	new	over
shallow	winter	lie	mean	old	under

Look at the word <u>narrow</u>. It was in the list at the start of this chapter.

Read this sentence:

> No one could walk through the <u>narrow</u> cave.

Which word means the OPPOSITE of <u>narrow</u>?

A wide

B slim

C deep

Does it sound like people can fit in the cave? No, it doesn't. It actually sounds like it is too thin. Now, look at the choices: <u>wide</u>, <u>slim</u>, or <u>deep</u>. Which one is the opposite of <u>thin</u>?

<u>Wide</u> is the opposite of <u>thin</u>. So, <u>wide</u> is the opposite of <u>narrow</u>. Answer **A** is right. Did you pick A?

Word Meaning

Activity: Opposite World

Pretend that there is a place called Opposite World. All things are backwards there. It is very odd. Red things are blue. Slow things are fast. Tall things are short.

Say you took a trip to Opposite World. You saw a big ant. You saw tiny buildings.

Your friends want to see the big ant! They want to see the tiny mountain too! To show them, you can draw a picture. It may look like this:

Look at this list. Read each question. What will each one look like in Opposite World?

In Opposite World…

what does a rainbow look like?

how does a cheetah move?

what does the desert look like?

how will the best field trip turn out?

what do your mom and dad look like?

how will your favorite music sound?

will your jokes be funny?

Now, draw pictures of two or three things from this list.

Chapter 14

Practice 2: Antonyms

ELA2R3 c

Read the passage. Then, answer the questions.

Grandma's Locket

Grandma <u>gave</u> me a locket for my birthday. It was very <u>shiny</u>. She said it was hers when she was <u>young</u>.

I love my new necklace. I will put a picture of Grandma <u>inside</u> the locket. That way, I will <u>always</u> think of her.

1 Which word is the OPPOSITE of <u>gave</u>?

   A showed

   B bought

   C took

2 Which word is the OPPOSITE of <u>shiny</u>?

   A bright

   B dull

   C pretty

3 Which word means the OPPOSITE of <u>young</u>?

   A old

   B little

   C scared

Word Meaning

4 Which word means the OPPOSITE of <u>inside</u>?

   A downside

   B upside

   C outside

5 Which word means the OPPOSITE of <u>always</u>?

   A never

   B sometimes

   C forever

HOMOPHONES

Homophones are words that sound the same. They are not spelled the same. And, they do not mean the same things.

For example, the words <u>which</u> and <u>witch</u> sound the same. But, they are not spelled the same. Also, they have different meanings. Look at how they can be used.

    Examples: <u>Which</u> candy are you going to choose?

                      The Wicked <u>Witch</u> of the West in *The Wizard of Oz* is mean.

Some other homophones are in this box:

> <u>die</u> and <u>dye</u>
> <u>night</u> and <u>knight</u>
> <u>to</u>, <u>too</u>, and <u>two</u>
> <u>their</u>, <u>there</u>, and <u>they're</u>
> <u>wear</u> and <u>where</u>
> <u>wood</u> and <u>would</u>

Can you think of more words that sound the same?

Chapter 14

HOMOGRAPHS

Homographs are words that are spelled the same. They mean different things. Some words that are spelled the same are not said the same way. But, some do sound the same.

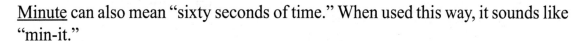

For example, the word <u>minute</u> can be used like this:

<u>Minute</u> can mean "very small." It sounds like "my-noot."

> The flea is a <u>minute</u> animal.

<u>Minute</u> can also mean "sixty seconds of time." When used this way, it sounds like "min-it."

> My sister can hold her breath for a <u>minute</u>.

Here are a few more:

Looks like this:	One meaning:	Another meaning:
Words that sound alike		
match	Your shirt and pants don't <u>match</u> today.	Get a <u>match</u> so we can light the candles on the cake.
mouse	Let me click the <u>mouse</u> to go to that Web site.	The little gray <u>mouse</u> ate the cheese.
pitcher	Grab the <u>pitcher</u> of lemonade.	Randy is the best <u>pitcher</u> on the team.
well	Wanda does not feel <u>well</u> today.	We get our water from a <u>well</u>.
Words that do not sound alike		
does	<u>Does</u> Mary like to dance?	We saw two female deer, called <u>does</u>, in the forest.
produce	This store never has fresh <u>produce</u> like lettuce or grapes.	He wants to <u>produce</u> a movie when he grows up.
wind	It is cold when the <u>wind</u> blows.	<u>Wind</u> up the clock to make sure it works.

Word Meaning

Practice 3: Homophones and Homographs
ELA2R3 c

Read the passage. Then, answer the questions.

Plane Ride

Vinnie is sitting in a <u>plane</u>. He can <u>hear</u> the engine from far away. It is so loud.

The pilot gave him a pin with wings on it. He sits <u>close</u> to the window. He wants to <u>see</u> everything.

When the plane takes off, Vinnie's ears pop. It feels funny. His dad gives him a <u>piece</u> of gum to chew. That helps his ears.

1. In this story, what does the word <u>plane</u> mean?

   A a flat surface

   B a machine that flies

   C to lift out of the water

2. Which word sounds like the word <u>hear</u>?

   A hair

   B hare

   C here

3. In this story, what does the word <u>close</u> mean?

   A near

   B to shut

   C ending

Chapter 14

4 Which word sounds like the word <u>see</u>?

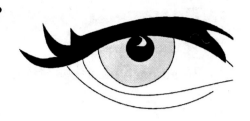

A saw

B ski

C sea

5 Which word sounds like the word <u>piece</u>?

A pace

B peace

C pears

CHAPTER 14 SUMMARY

Synonyms are similar words. They have the same meanings.

Antonyms are opposite words. They have different meanings.

Homophones are words that sound the same. They have different spellings and meanings.

Homographs are words that are spelled the same. They have different meanings. Many words that are spelled the same also sound alike. But, some do not.

Word Meaning

CHAPTER 14 REVIEW

ELA2R3 b, c

Read each passage. Then, answer the questions.

The Moon

You can see the moon at <u>night</u>. It is not as <u>bright</u> as the sun. It is big, but not as big as the earth.

The moon moves around the earth. The sun's light makes the moon shine at night. The moon goes through phases. That means we can only see <u>parts</u> of it at a time.

When it is full, we see the <u>whole</u> moon. When the moon is too dark to see, it's called a new moon.

1. Which word means the OPPOSITE of <u>night</u>?

    A day

    B week

    C month

2. In this passage, what does the word <u>bright</u> mean?

    A smart

    B shiny

    C colorful

3. In this passage, what word means the same as <u>parts</u>?

    A to spread

    B pieces

    C leaving

Chapter 14

4 Which word sounds the same as <u>whole</u>?

A hail

B heal

C hole

Writing in Cursive

Ward has trouble writing in cursive. It is very <u>hard</u> for him. He has to practice a lot.

He can't get the loops just <u>right</u>. His teacher helps him. His mom helps him.

Ward wants to do it by <u>himself</u>. He works on his name. He writes it <u>over</u> and over again. Finally, it looks like it should.

Ward is very <u>proud</u>. He can <u>write</u> in cursive. He shows his mom and his teacher. They knew he could do it.

5 In this story, what does the word <u>hard</u> mean?

A not soft

B difficult

C strict

6 What word means the same as <u>right</u>?

A wrong

B complete

C correct

Word Meaning

7 What word means the OPPOSITE of <u>over</u>?

A under

B beside

C top

8 In this story, what does the word <u>proud</u> mean?

A happy

B important

C rude

9 Which word does NOT sound the same as the word <u>write</u>?

A right

B rate

C rite

10 Which sentence BEST fits the picture?

A The corn harvest is stored in the <u>pen</u>.

B That <u>pen</u> is big enough for the herd.

C Use the <u>pen</u> to write your name.

Chapter 14

11 Which sentence fits the picture?

A The soldier <u>bows</u> before the queen.

B My sister wears <u>bows</u> in her hair.

C Some hunters use <u>bows</u> and arrows.

12 Which two uses of <u>can</u> mean the same thing?

> **1.** Heather keeps her money in a <u>can</u>.
>
> **2.** <u>Can</u> you count to one hundred?
>
> **3.** That <u>can</u> of soda tastes good.

A 1 and 3

B 1 and 2

C 2 and 3

Word Meaning

Georgia 2nd Grade CRCT in Reading Practice Test 1

This test is based on the Georgia Performance Standards for Reading and adheres to the sample question format provided by the Georgia Department of Education for the Reading Criterion-Referenced Competency Test.

Today, you will be taking a test that is like the CRCT. Your teacher will tell you how to mark the answers.

Here are some things to remember:

1. Read each passage carefully.

2. Read each question or sample. Then, choose the best answer.

3. Choose only one answer for each question. If you change an answer, be sure to erase your old answer completely.

4. Don't spend too much time on one question. If you do not know an answer, come back to it at the end.

5. After taking the test, you or your teacher should score it.

Practice Test 1

First, read each passage. Then, choose the best answer for each question.

Little Doctor

Ray wants to be a doctor when he grows up. He likes to help people.

Sandy fell down one day, and Ray helped her. He got her some ice for her knee. Carl got a paper cut on his finger. Ray got a bandage to stop the bleeding.

Ray likes to help animals too. He saw a bird with a hurt wing. He took care of the bird until it could fly again. He found a stray cat. He fed it and brushed its fur.

Ray will be a good doctor. He cares for people and animals.

1 What does Ray want to be when he grows up?   ELA2R4 i

  A a dentist

  B a teacher

  C a doctor

2 What could NOT be true about this passage?   ELA2R4 f

  A People like Ray.

  B Animals talk to Ray.

  C Ray is very helpful.

3 What is the BEST summary of this story?   ELA2R4 e

  A Ray cares for people and animals.

  B Ray teases people and animals.

  C Ray wants to be an animal.

4 Which word means "more than one?" ELA2R4 p

   A its

   B likes

   C animals

5 Ray sees someone fall on the playground. What will Ray MOST LIKELY do? ELA2R4 b

   A He will go see if the person is hurt.

   B He will laugh at the person who fell.

   C He will play kickball with his friends.

6 What sentence is true about Ray? ELA2R4 l

   A Ray is mean to strangers.

   B Ray is nice to everyone.

   C Ray is bored at school.

Practice Test 1

7 What graphic BEST fits the story? ELA2R4 g

A

B

C

Baseball Uniforms

A baseball player wears a uniform. This shows which team he plays for. Each uniform has the team's name on it.

The player's last name goes on the back of the shirt. Each player has a number. It goes on the back of the shirt too. Some uniforms have a small number on the front too.

Baseball players also wear pants, socks, and a cap. Some have a glove. They wear special shoes called spikes. They have little pins on the bottom. These help players run better.

Each team has <u>certain</u> colors. Players wear white when they play in their own city. They wear a dark color when they play in another city.

8 Where is the player's number NOT found?

A on the back

B on the front

C on the pants

9 Why do baseball players wear spikes?

A to help them swing their bats

B to help them slide better

C to help them run better

Practice Test 1

10 Why did the author MOST LIKELY write this passage?

A to explain when teams wear uniforms

B to describe how baseball uniforms look

C to teach someone how to play baseball

ELA2R4 o

11 This story is a good example of

A a poem.

B an article.

C a fable.

ELA2R4 m

12 In this passage, what does the word <u>certain</u> mean?

A having confidence

B a clear winner

C specific ones

ELA2R3 b

13 What is NOT part of a uniform?

A bat

B cap

C glove

ELA2R4 i

14 What word sounds the same as the word <u>wear</u>?

A were

B where

C war

ELA2R3 c

Georgia 2nd Grade CRCT in Reading

Olivia Learns to Play the Piano

Olivia likes music. She wants to play the piano. She has to learn how to play first. She asks her parents if she can take lessons. They say yes.

Her mom takes her to Mrs. Bell's house. Mrs. Bell is a music teacher. She has played the piano for years. She has a piano at her house. She teaches many kids how to play. She has been doing that for twelve years. She is very <u>adept</u> at playing the piano.

First, Mrs. Bell tells about the keys. She teaches Olivia why some keys are white and why some are black. Then, she shows her how to hold her hands on the keys. She shows where the pedals are. They are near the bottom of the piano. They help to hold notes. That means notes can play longer.

Next, they talk about what a beat is. It is a way to count time in music. Each note has a number of beats. That tells how long to hold the note. Olivia listens to Mrs. Bell. She wants to learn all she can.

Mrs. Bell gives Olivia this chart to teach her the first few notes.

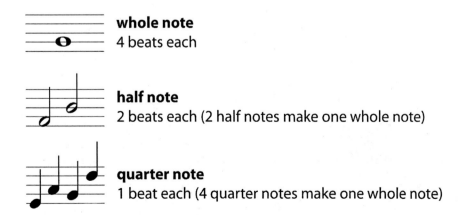

209

Practice Test 1

15 Where is this story set?

A a doctor's office

B a piano store

C Mrs. Bell's house

ELA2R4 l

16 What will MOST LIKELY happen next?

A Olivia will practice what she has learned.

B Olivia will stop playing the piano.

C Olivia will start playing the violin instead.

ELA2R4 b

17 Why does Olivia listen to Mrs. Bell?

A She wants to win a prize.

B She wants to learn how to play.

C She wants to repeat what Mrs. Bell says.

ELA2R4 k

18 What is the BEST way to sum up this story?

A Olivia learns how to listen.

B Olivia uses her good manners.

C Olivia starts piano lessons.

ELA2R4 e

19 In the chart, how long is a whole note?

A 1 beat

B 2 beats

C 4 beats

ELA2R4 g

20 What is the first thing Mrs. Bell teaches Olivia?

A why the keys are black and white

B how to hold her hands on the keys

C why the pedals are near the ground

ELA2R4 d

21 In this story, what does the word <u>adept</u> mean?

A brave

B skilled

C forgetful

Manny the Anteater

Manny is an anteater. He eats ants. He has a long tongue. It is almost as long as a person's arm! It is very sticky. His tongue helps him get ants. Some ants hide in tree trunks. Manny uses his tongue to reach the ants.

Manny also likes to play soccer with his friends. He is the goalie on his school team. Last year, his team won a trophy. This year, they need to win one more game to get a trophy.

Today is game day. His team plays very hard. They are winning. Then, the other team gets to make a free shot. Manny has to block the ball. The anteater from the other team kicks the ball. Manny blocks it. His team wins the game! They all celebrate with an ant feast.

22 What in this story could NOT be true about anteaters?

A They have sticky tongues.

B They eat ants.

C They play soccer.

23 What is MOST LIKELY the author's reason for writing this story?

A to explain to readers how anteaters use their tongues

B to entertain readers with a made-up story about anteaters

C to teach readers how to best block a soccer ball

Practice Test 1

24 What happens after Manny's team wins the game?   ELA2R4 l

    A They have an ant feast.

    B They go home and sleep.

    C They do not win the game.

25 What is the OPPOSITE of the word <u>win</u>?   ELA2R3 c

    A tie

    B lose

    C wave

26 What spot does Manny play in soccer?   ELA2R4 d

    A goalie

    B forward

    C referee

27 What is the main idea of this story?   ELA2R4 i

    A Manny likes to eat bugs and plants.

    B Manny helps his team win the game.

    C Manny does not play by the rules.

28 Why does Manny's team win the game?   ELA2R4 k

    A Manny makes the winning goal.

    B Manny runs out of time to score.

    C Manny blocks the other team's shot.

Money, Money, Money

Little Tommy gets some money
When he does his chores.
Little Tommy is <u>greedy</u>, though.
He always wants some more.

He does not spend his money.
He says there is no need.
He crams a box with more and more
Because he's filled with greed.

His friends ask to borrow money;
Little Tommy says "No way!"
"Get your own money," he says.
His friends don't know what to say.

Little Tommy once lost some money
Down a gutter near his school.
His friends came to help the sad boy
Who was sorry he'd been so cruel.

Practice Test 1

29 This passage is an example of

   A a poem.

   B an article.

   C a fable.

30 Which sentence describes Little Tommy?

   A He walks fast on his way to school.

   B He likes to have lots of money.

   C He loves to play games with friends.

31 In this passage, what does the word <u>greedy</u> mean?

   A always wants more

   B never wants anything

   C good at doing chores

32 What does this passage teach?

   A Being mean is a way to make friends.

   B Money is the most important thing.

   C Do not be selfish with what you have.

33 How will Little Tommy MOST LIKELY act from now on?

   A He will be mean to his friends.

   B He will be nice to his friends.

   C He will get new friends.

34 What does Little Tommy do with his money?

   A just keeps it in a box

   B buys things he needs

   C gets presents for friends

Georgia 2nd Grade CRCT in Reading

35 How many word parts does the word <u>helped</u> have?

ELA2R4 p

A 1

B 2

C 3

Frankie and the Frog

Frankie walks to the pond every day. He likes to throw rocks. He throws them very far. One day, Frankie goes to the edge of the pond. He sees a creature swimming around. He looks closer. It is a tadpole.

Frankie scoops up the baby frog. He takes it home in a cup of lake water. Mom lets him put the tadpole in a fishbowl. The tadpole will grow into a frog, and Frankie will have a pet frog. Mom boils some lettuce. Frankie feeds his tadpole.

Frankie has to wait a long time for it to be a frog. It could take a few months. Soon, the tadpole will <u>sprout</u> legs. Then, it will lose its tail. Finally, it will be a frog!

Frog Life Cycle

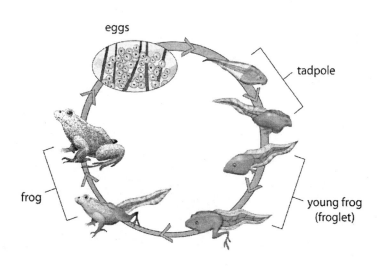

Practice Test 1

36 This passage is MOST LIKELY what kind of writing? ELA2R4 m

A a story

B a fable

C a poem

37 In this passage, what does the word <u>sprout</u> mean? ELA2R3 b

A to be a child

B to remove pieces

C to start growing

38 If the frog began talking, how would that change the story? ELA2R4 f

A It would have more characters.

B It would be a made-up story.

C It would explain more about frogs.

39 In the diagram, what is the second stage in a frog life cycle? ELA2R4 g

A Eggs

B Tadpole

C Frog

40 Which sentence BEST sums up this story? ELA2R4 e

A Frankie finds a frog and will keep it as a pet.

B Frankie finds a pond that he can throw rocks in.

C Frankie finds a tadpole that will grow into a frog.

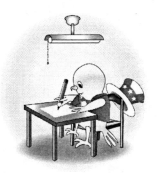

Georgia 2nd Grade CRCT in Reading Practice Test 2

This test is based on the Georgia Performance Standards for Reading and adheres to the sample question format provided by the Georgia Department of Education for the Reading Criterion-Referenced Competency Test.

Today, you will be taking a test that is like the CRCT. Your teacher will tell you how to mark the answers.

Here are some things to remember:

1. Read each passage carefully.

2. Read each question or sample. Then, choose the best answer.

3. Choose only one answer for each question. If you change an answer, be sure to erase your old answer completely.

4. Don't spend too much time on one question. If you do not know an answer, come back to it at the end.

5. After taking the test, you or your teacher should score it.

Practice Test 2

Read each passage. Then, choose the best answer for each question.

Helping

adapted from a poem by Emily Dickinson

If I can heal one breaking heart,

If I can <u>cool</u> your pain,

Then I've played my little part

And have not lived in vain.

If I can help one <u>fainting</u> bird

Into his nest again,

Then I know I've proved my worth

And have not lived in vain.

1. Which word has the same ending sound as <u>worth</u>?

   A earth

   B curse

   C shirts

2. The speaker MOST LIKELY has a friend who is

   A sad.

   B tall.

   C mean.

3 In this story, the word <u>cool</u> means

   A trendy.

   B lessen.

   C chill.

4 Which word rhymes with <u>pain</u>?

   A heart

   B part

   C vain

5 The speaker wants to

   A become a heart doctor.

   B make a friend feel better.

   C build bird nests.

6 How would the speaker MOST LIKELY feel about helping a friend?

   A bored

   B happy

   C scared

7 Which word sounds the same as <u>vain</u>?

   A vend

   B vine

   C vein

LeBron James Has Many Jobs

LeBron James plays basketball. He is one of the best players ever. People say he can fly like a bird. He has been <u>famous</u> since he was in high school. He is paid a lot of money for being a good player.

His team pays him money. But, LeBron knows he will not play sports all his life. He is smart. He finds other jobs to do.

He works very hard. People pay him to star in ads. He tries to help Nike sell shoes. He also wants to make movies.

LeBron makes money by being <u>strong</u> and fast. More importantly, he makes money by being smart.

8 Which sentence is NOT true about LeBron?

A He works very hard.

B He finds other jobs to do.

C He can fly like a bird.

9 What does LeBron want to do someday?

A go to high school

B become famous

C make movies

10 Which word means the OPPOSITE of <u>famous</u>?

A unknown

B popular

C special

11 The author wrote this passage to

A tell about LeBron's life.

B show ways to make money.

C teach how to play sports.

12 How many word parts are in the word <u>strong</u>?

A 1

B 2

C 3

13 Why will LeBron NOT play sports all his life?

A Playing basketball will be a crime.

B He will get too old someday.

C The world will run out of money.

14 In this passage, LeBron James stars in ads for

A Reebok.

B Adidas.

C Nike.

15 Which sentence BEST sums up this passage?

A LeBron is one of the best basketball players ever.

B LeBron makes money by doing many jobs well.

C LeBron has been famous since he was in high school.

Gardening with Grandpa

Grandpa grows plants in his garden. He has strawberries and peas. He has roses and melons. There is even a plant that smells bad. It smells like a monster's toothbrush. I stay away from that plant.

Practice Test 2

Grandpa <u>showed</u> me how to garden. It's not very hard. It's fun.

One part of the garden is mine. I have a tomato plant. I also have a green pepper plant. It's my job to take care of them. I water them. And, I pull weeds out of the dirt. Weeds grow so fast. Weeds could hurt my plants.

My tomatoes and peppers are <u>ripe</u>. They are ready to eat. We take them inside.

We cut them up and put them in a big bowl. We add onions and a little hot sauce. We just made salsa! My cousins all try it. Everyone loves it.

16 What is one way to help a plant live?

   A Add hot sauce.

   B Water it.

   C Cut it up.

17 What would happen if nobody pulled weeds?

   A Weeds would hurt other plants.

   B Weeds would become ripe.

   C Weeds would not grow very fast.

> He <u>showed</u> me how to garden.

18 When did Grandpa show the author how to garden?

   A in the past

   B right now

   C in the future

19 This story is about ELA2R4 e

   A making salsa.

   B learning to garden.

   C plants that smell funny.

20 Which sentence is made up? ELA2R4 f

   A We cut them up and put them in a big bowl.

   B Grandpa showed me how to garden.

   C A plant smells like a monster's toothbrush.

21 In this story, which of these is used to make salsa? ELA2R4 i

   A strawberries

   B onions

   C melons

22 In this story, the word <u>ripe</u> means ELA2R3 d

   A cut into pieces.

   B taken inside.

   C ready to eat.

Animals and Mirrors

There is a test to see how smart an animal is. It's called the mirror test. It is used to see if an animal can use a mirror.

The test goes like this. An animal is shown a mirror. The animal sees itself. How does it react?

Most animals cannot <u>identify</u> that they are looking at their own face. They just think they see some other animal. They may try to play with it. Dogs may bark. Cats may get scared.

Practice Test 2

Some animals can learn. They can know what they are looking at. An elephant can spot itself in a mirror. A dolphin can too. Some apes like to see how they look.

This is a way to tell that these are very smart animals.

23 This article was written to   ELA2R4 o

    A explain a test for animals.

    B entertain people who like mirrors.

    C describe what animals look like.

24 Why might a dog bark when it sees a mirror?   ELA2R4 k

    A It thinks it sees a mean person.

    B It thinks it sees another dog.

    C It hates things made of glass.

25 Which animal can learn to look at itself in a mirror?   ELA2R4 l

    A a snake

    B a cricket

    C a dolphin

26 What are scientists LIKELY to do in the future?   ELA2R4 b

    A Try the mirror test on more animals.

    B Stop doing the mirror test.

    C Teach dolphins how to ride bikes.

27 In this story, the word <u>identify</u> means   ELA2R3 d

    A sing.

    B see.

    C swim.

How to Make a Pompom

Pompoms are fun! You can cheer with them. They make great party favors. They are also easy to make. First, you need to get these things:

2 sheets of tissue paper
1 empty toilet paper roll
color construction paper
scissors
clear tape
stapler

1. **Make a handle:** Wrap construction paper around the toilet paper roll. Tape it in a few places to make it stay on. This is your handle.

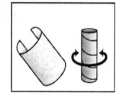

2. **Make strips:** Fold the tissue paper in half. Cut the tissue paper into long, thin strips. Each strip should be as <u>thin</u> as your finger. Don't cut all the way to the end. Let the strips hold together on one end.

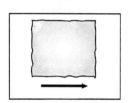

3. **Put strips in the handle:** Put the uncut end of the strips in the handle. It should only go in a couple of inches.

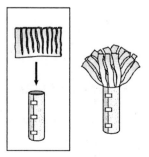

Practice Test 2

4. **Attach strips:** Staple the strips into the handle. This will hold the end of the strips in the handle. Now you have a pompom.

5. **Cheer!**

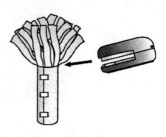

28 Why should you staple the top of the handle?

   A to cut the paper into strips

   B to hold all the strips in

   C to get construction paper

ELA2R4 d

29 Who would MOST LIKELY use pompoms?

   A football player

   B cheerleader

   C teacher

ELA2R4 l

30 To make a pompom, you need

   A four kinds of things.

   B five kinds of things.

   C six kinds of things.

ELA2R4 i

31 The author of this passage wanted to

   A cut tissue paper into strips.

   B sell empty toilet paper rolls.

   C tell how to make a pompom.

ELA2R4 o

32 Which word means the OPPOSITE of thin?

   A slim

   B thick

   C long

ELA2R3 c

33 Wrapping construction paper around a roll makes

   A a handle.

   B a pompom.

   C scissors.

ELA2R4 k

History of Guitars

Do you know where guitars came from? Here is a timeline:

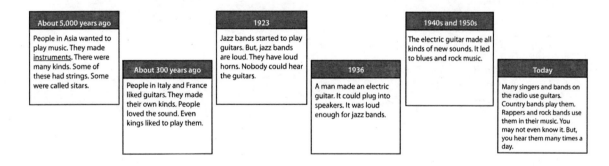

34 Which of these events happened FIRST?

   A Jazz bands started to play guitar.

   B People in France made guitars.

   C A man made an electric guitar.

ELA2R4 g

35 Which is the BEST way to sum up this article?

   A Many bands use guitars these days.

   B People in Asia made guitars.

   C Guitars have a long history.

ELA2R4 e

36 Which event was the MOST recent?

A People in Asia made instruments.

B A new guitar led to blues music.

C Rappers used guitars in their songs.

37 In this timeline, the word <u>instrument</u> means

A something for playing music.

B a friend who likes to help.

C a tool for making strings.

38 When did a man invent the electric guitar?

A in 1923

B in 1936

C in the 1940s

39 Where were sitars first made?

A Italy

B France

C Asia

40 In the future, people will MOST LIKELY

A find new ways to play guitar.

B send all the guitars back to Asia.

C make kings stop playing guitars.

A
antonym 191, 197
article 77
asking questions 87, 88, 93
author purpose 17, 28
  to describe 23, 28
  to entertain 26, 28
  to explain 18, 28
  to teach 21, 28

B
basket organizer 133
beginning of a story 61, 64

C
cause 107, 111
cause and effect 107, 109, 110, 111
character 53, 54, 64
chart 116, 121
compare 54, 64
compound word 161, 162, 165
context clue 145, 146, 154, 188

D
detail 82, 83
diagram 124
dictionary 150, 151, 152, 154

E
effect 107, 111
end of a story 62, 64
events in a story 60

F
fable 36, 47, 77
fact 69, 74, 77
fiction 69, 74
folktale 38, 39, 47

G
glossary 152, 154
graphic 115, 116
graphic organizer 131, 139

H
homograph 195, 197
homophone 194, 197

I
illustration 116
infer 79, 83
inference 72, 74
informational text 45, 47, 77

K
key words 110

L
line chart 122

M
made-up story 33, 38, 47, 69, 77, 98
main idea 77, 79, 82, 83, 90
middle of a story 61, 64
multiple meaning 148, 151, 154

O
opposite word 191, 197
order of events 109

P
parts of a story 61, 62
pie chart 121
plot 60, 64
poem 41, 47, 77
predict 98, 102

R
rhyming words 42
root 157, 165, 169, 176
root word 161

S
s rule 169, 173, 175, 182
same word 188, 197
setting 57, 58, 64
sorting 131

sorting basket 139
story basics 87
story train 136, 139
summary 89, 90, 93
synonym 188, 197

T

thesaurus 153, 154
time order 135, 139
timeline 135, 139

V

Venn diagram 132, 139

W

word ending 175, 176, 178, 181, 182
word part 169, 175, 182
word root 157
word spelling 181, 182